# Fixing The Broken, Without Being Broken- Book 1

BY: JEROME REDD

# FIXING THE BROKEN
## WITHOUT BEING BROKEN
### TURNING ON THE LIGHT, SO THAT CHANGE CAN TAKE PLACE

**JEROME REDD**

Copyright © 2022 by Trient Press

All rights reserved. No part of this publication may be reproduced, distributed, or transmitted in any form or by any means, including photocopying, recording, or other mechanical methods, without the prior written permission of the publisher, except in the case of brief quotations embodied in critical reviews and certain other noncommercial uses permitted by copyright law. For permission requests, write to the publisher, addressed "Attention: Permissions Coordinator," at the address below.

Criminal copyright infringement, including infringement without monetary gain, is investigated by the FBI and is punishable by up to five years in federal prison and a fine of $250,000.

Except for the original story material written by the author, all songs, song titles, and lyrics mentioned in the novel Fixing The Broker, Without Being Broken- Book 1 are the exclusive property of the respective artists, songwriters, and copyright holder.

Trient Press
3375 S Rainbow Blvd
#81710, SMB 13135
Las Vegas,NV 89180

Ordering Information:

Quantity sales. Special discounts are available on quantity purchases by corporations, associations, and others. For details, contact the publisher at the address above.

Orders by U.S. trade bookstores and wholesalers. Please contact Trient Press: Tel: (775) 996-3844; or visit www.trientpress.com.

Printed in the United States of America

Publisher's Cataloging-in-Publication data

Author Name- Redd, Jerome

A title of a book : Fixing The Broken, Without Being Broken- Book 1

| ISBN | |
|---|---|
| Paperback | 978-1-955198-49-3 |
| E-book | 978-1-955198-50-9 |
| Hard Cover | 978-1-955198-46-2 |

# Contents

Dedication
Foreword
Introduction
**Volume I**

| | |
|---|---|
| CHAPTER 1 | It Was Just Supposed To Be A Short Train Ride |
| CHAPTER 2 | The Short Version |
| CHAPTER 3 | Stuck Between The Short And Long Version |
| CHAPTER 4 | The Dirty Laundry, Please |
| CHAPTER 5 | Before I Could Tell Their Story, I Had To Tell His-Story |
| CHAPTER 6 | The 6th Grade Teacher Who Changed My Life |
| CHAPTER 7 | My Journey Beyond The Brokenness |
| CHAPTER 8 | The Long Version Set-Up |
| CHAPTER 9 | You Can't Function Without Properly Calibrating Your GPS. Was It Six-Figures Or Go Figure |
| CHAPTER 10 | The Right Place, At The Right Time? Yea Right! |
| CHAPTER 11 | So What Have I Gotten Myself Into |
| CHAPTER 12 | Expectations |

## Volume II
### You Know How To Survive. I Want You To Learn How To Live

| | |
|---|---|
| *CHAPTER 13* | Forget The Appetizer. Are You Ready For The Entrée |
| *CHAPTER 14* | The Big Three |
| *CHAPTER 15* | So What About My Opinion |

## Volume III
### Group Sessions/One-on-Ones

| | |
|---|---|
| *CHAPTER 16* | Let's Talk Money, Drugs and/or Sex |

## Volume IV
### Finding The Missing Pieces, Nugget By Nugget

| | |
|---|---|
| *Nuggets* | Nuggets 1-3 |
| *CHAPTER 17* | Last Shall Be First |
| *CHAPTER 18* | The Thought For Today |
| *CHAPTER 19* | Don't Forget How To Dream |
| *CHAPTER 20* | No He Didn't. Yes He Did |
| *CHAPTER 21* | Did You Reach All? Sergeant Redd, You Saved My Life |
| *CHAPTER 22* | He Wasn't Ready Or Was He |
| *Poem* | Are You Really Listening |
| *CHAPTER 23* | We All Need An ROI |

**Connect With Me**

# Dedication

THE GIVER OF GRACE:

First, I would be remiss if I didn't thank my Father, which art in Heaven. By the saving grace of His only begotten Son, this book(s) finally got published. When I started writing this book some fifteen years ago, I thought it was going to be one book. By the time God was finished with me, it turned into a 3-book series on Fixing The Broken.

BOOK 1: Turning On The Light, So Change Can Take Place

This book is dedicated to all those young people who I have had the extreme pleasure of meeting and being a part of their lives. I am also pleased so many of them had a direct impact and positive outcome on my life. They gave me the ultimate boost to never quit and never give up. It was this type of inspiration that finally got my inner thoughts onto paper. I also hope what they gave to me was only an example of what they had and passed on to many more in need. I pray I was not the exception, but the rule.

BOOK 2: The Unsuspecting Impact

This book is for all of those Mr. Posey's out there who love teaching and love kids. Mr. Posey was my 6th grade teacher. Mr. Posey, you saved my life. This is also for those parents, administrators, coaches, mentors, care-givers, etc., whose ultimate responsibility is to take care of and watch over someone. In Book 1, I showed you what happened between me and in the one-on-one interactions with the kids. In Book 2, I explain the behind-the-scenes actions, the input that impacted and even those who tried to sabotage at times, everything that I was working for. I also provided some tips and attributes to remember as you navigate your path with the broken. Book 1 was the good. Book 2 was the bad and the ugly. Put on your seat-belt.

BOOK 3: The Poetic Journey

Book 3 came out of default. If you've read Books 1&2, you will see that I poured my heart and soul into this project and these kids. In addition, I wasn't looking for anything in return other than their success when they returned to New York City. What occurred as a direct impact and input of these kids was me publishing 3 books of poetry. Along with these 3 books they inspired me to write, is also some additional poetry written and included in Book 3 as well. I am speechless.

My Faithful Supporters:

These books are also dedicated to all of you who have patiently waited year, after year, after year for me, until I finally got it done. Thank you. Enjoy.

# Forward

There is so much that I can say about Jerome Redd and I will actually do it in the foreword. Before I tell you how good this book is, I need to first tell you how good Jerome is as a person. He is a gift to mankind and I am very grateful for him. Honestly, he is a gift to mankind and you need to follow him and support him for as long as he lives.

I don't know many things in life, but I do have one fundamental understanding that leads and guides me to prosperity each day: We are all connected. This is how I met Jerome. I was walking past him at a Les Brown Conference and a jolt of lighting rushed through my legs and made me stop. I can't explain it, but I knew that if I kept walking past Jerome, that I would have missed out on an opportunity to meet greatness. Boy, am I glad that I was right. Jerome has changed my life. His kindness and his presence are exactly what driven and busy people like me need. People like Jerome remind me that life is not meant to be too fast or too rushed. It is meant to be shared with others.

Enter, Jerome's 3-book series: "Fixing The Broken, Without Being Broken" (Book 1) (Turning On The Light, So That Change Can Take Place), "Fixing The Broken, Without Being Broken" (Book 2) (The Unsuspecting Impact), and "Fixing The Broken, Without Being Broken" (Book 3) (The Poetic Journey).

I have had the luxury to read each of these books and I am forever changed by them. There is a sweet retreat in each of these books. I am reminded of a book that says, "If you are faithful to the few, you will be ruler over many." Dear Reader, I can assure you, these books are faithful to the brokenhearted and I fully expect for Jerome to reap a full harvest from his faithfulness.

In Book1, Jerome writes, "Nobody pushed me or told me, 'Hey Jerome, you have got to write this book. Come on dude, let's get it done.' That didn't happen." You see, no one had to push Jerome to be faithful to the brokenhearted. He was led by something far greater than all of us.

There is another section in which Jerome writes: "Although HIV isn't as rampant as it once was, it has and still is leaving its mark on our society. Too many young people and adults are having unprotected sex with some crazy results. Forget the ethical, moral and spiritual implications. We aren't even asking one another, have you been tested? And, if we do ask, we don't check. Somebody is asleep at the wheel." It is at this point in the book in which Jerome takes off the kid gloves and gets into our hearts and pulls at our morals. He reminded me that I have not done enough to help this world. None of us have.

Book 1 is splendid. I won't ruin the other books for you, but I do want you to know that you are in for an emotional ride that will not disappoint you. Jerome, you are my brother for life. I am so grateful that I have met you. I consider you my friend and my coach. Although I coach you, my friend, you have given far more value into my life than I have ever given you. It is because of you I can remember to take time for people, no matter who they are and what they have done. I love you with all my heart and I am very happy the world gets to love you like I do.

Best,

Antonio T. Smith, Jr.

Mentee and Mentor of Jerome Redd.

# Introduction

**The Author**

Before I give you any background about this story, let me first give you a little background about the person who comprised this story. He is very different and yet, very ordinary. He is extremely strong and yet, very vulnerable. He will give of his last, without hesitation. He is always learning and yet, very intelligent. The evolution of time has caused him to see the broken; experience the broken; fix the broken; and even become the broken. His carousel of evolving titles makes him uniquely positioned to address this issue of brokenness. But, is he qualified to answer that $64,000-dollar question? "Can I fix the broken, without being broken?" Now, that still remains to be seen.

**The Question is?**

So, some of you may be asking the pressing question, what is the purpose of this book and why did it need to be written in the first place? Before I answer that question, I would first like to ask you to go back and look at the title again. Then ask yourself the following question(s)? How many of you know a child, a student, a neighbor, a co-worker, a friend, a family member who is or has been broken? How many of you have witnessed or personally experienced the results of such brokenness? How many of you after having seen or experienced this brokenness, made a heart-felt attempt to fix it? On the other hand, in trying to fix the broken, you decided to abandon your attempt or not even try to help in the first place. Have you ever in your attempt to try to fix the broken, quickly realize that you were way in over your head? So, as a result, you didn't even try to do any fixing, period. Do any of these questions hit home or sound somewhat familiar? I hope so.

Now let me attempt to try to answer your question, Why? About twenty years ago in up-state New York over a period of about seven years, something happened to me and with me, involving the broken, that some might even call miraculous. I found myself in a contradictory place where there was a lot of sadness and brokenness and not a lot of ways to fix or change this. When I finally walked away after seven years, I also felt pretty good about the help that I was able to give, which made a big difference. At the time, I was also ignorant and had no clue as to what I had really accomplished against such insurmountable odds, until much later.

It wasn't until about fifteen years later surrounding a quiet train ride back to New York City that I truly realized what had taken place; what I had done and what an enormous impact I had on the lives of some unsuspecting kids and adults as well. This impact was truly life-changing.

This first book about the broken looks at the background of this story and where it takes place. It is focused mainly on the one-on-one exchanges I had as I encountered these broken vessels. I also explain and elaborate on the type of techniques I used to implement and stimulate a change in these young people's lives. Although I didn't realize this at first, I also later discovered what they in-turn, had passed on to me. Without this small innocent revelation, I believe this book would have never been written. These kids literally changed my life, forever.

As a retired Senior Sergeant from the United States Army, I have traveled all over the world. I am the author of three published books of poetry. I've also been exposed to a unique point of view when it comes to our youth today. In addition, I also have had opportunities to speak with and interact with a number of parents and care-givers over the years. I then got to personally work at this boot-camp in upstate New York for seven years. It became one of the best jobs at which I have ever had the pleasure to work. Now, let's fast forward twenty years. I have also personally observed, listened to others, and watched on the news how bad our country is getting as a whole, on a daily basis. If I listen strictly to the news, our children today are in a lot of trouble. That might be true. Although I would have to agree that something definitely needs to be done, our troubled country is not my chosen area of expertise.

You need to be checking with others for answers in this particular field. With that being said, I have had some personal interaction and motivating experiences when it directly comes to our youth and to those who are considered troubled youth. I've never been licensed or an official clinician of juvenile cognitive behavior. Let me tell you, it wasn't until I did some real soul-searching and reflecting that I came to realize that maybe I do have something to offer by way of a real change. Maybe I do have something to say or contribute that could make an overall difference. Nevertheless, my self-talk then took over. "You know for a fact that you made a difference some twenty years ago at that boot-camp in upstate New York. What has really changed since then? What are you lacking now that would prevent you from giving input and insight into this clouded and convoluted matter of brokenness?" As I truly searched my inner man, I could not find an answer that would keep me silent. It was at this moment that I knew I needed to tell this very story to those who are out there working with the broken. I also knew that I needed to find a way for me to get back into that saddle again. I needed to find a way to get back to twenty years earlier, when I was working with these kids. When I finally found the courage to tell this pressing story to a friend about brokenness, I thought at the time it was for him and him only. I thought my confession alone about my boot-camp experience would suffice. It wasn't until later that I realized and knew that this hunger needed to go into a book for everyone to see and learn from. It was not just for a chosen few to experience.

When I decided to resign from that job working with at-risk kids some twenty years ago, I felt good about what I had done for them. Nevertheless, I also felt broken that I had to depart the facility under circumstances to me that were less than what you might call favorable. When I reflect on all the wonderful achievements which occurred during my tenure at that facility, my need to step down was so unbelievable. Because of me, the staff, gave the kids additional time to their sentence. The kids became the sacrifice for me. I had no choice but to resign. With this troubling departure, I decided I would take that particular piece of my life's history and place it or should I say, hide it away so that I didn't have to face or deal with it in my future. This was such a sad commentary, considering that I had such a successful tenure at that place. If it weren't for the fact that I really cared about the people, the kids and the value of true friendship, this story might still be in my head and never been put to paper.

Now, here is the real crazy part of why this book ever saw the light of day. I got set-up. A very intelligent man; a highly successful man; a man who I have the utmost respect for, was at a crossroads in his life. He had run into a problem and could not come up with a solution. For some crazy unknown reason, he thought I might just have the answer that he was looking for.

    He and I were taking an Amtrak train from Baltimore, Maryland to New York City and back, for a business trip. In conjunction with business discussions, he and I have always had very thought-provoking, intellectually stimulating mental exchanges when we talk. Since our business trips alone are few, I cherish every opportunity to spend some one-on-one time with this guy. In my lifetime, there has not been another individual who stimulates and provokes me to go where he intellectually takes me. Needless to say, every chance I get to have a conversation with him is a mentally exhilarating joy ride. I didn't expect our trip to New York to be any different than previous trips. By the time, I returned from this trip, I could not believe what had happened on this trip. There was no warning or preparation for the convergence that I was about to embrace. There were no signs or landmarks posted anywhere to let me know what type of voyage this was going to be. Someone should have told me to put on a protective suit and strap on my seat-belt. Why? Because it was going to be an interesting ride; a bumpy ride; the ride of my life.

    So, the narrative that you are about to embark upon didn't start out as a book. It started out with me realizing that someone who I respected needed a hard answer to a hard question and decided to turn to me for a possible solution. Although I had some of the hard answers, I wasn't sure at the time if these would be the answers he needed. Nevertheless, by the time I finished speaking, I knew I was right on target and had delivered the right answers. In addition, I gave him far more facts and information than either one of us expected. It was in this precise time and at this precise moment I finally realized that when I was previously in New York, with those kids that I had fixed the broken. Yet, I had not become broken myself. This was an amazing revelation. It was also at this point that I knew I had to write about it and not just talk about it. So, this fixing the broken, without being broken, started off as nothing more than a simple train ride, with the need to answer a very interesting question.

By the time that simple Amtrack train ride was over, I don't know what happened or how it happened. But let me tell you, something happened. If I haven't mentioned it already, something really happened.

# VOLUME I

## All Aboard

# FIXING THE BROKEN
## WITHOUT BEING BROKEN
### TURNING ON THE LIGHT, SO THAT CHANGE CAN TAKE PLACE

**JEROME REDD**

# The Background:

# Chapter 1:
# It Was Just Supposed To Be A Short Train Ride

As the Amtrak train departed the Baltimore Penn station headed to the Big Apple for our presentation, I was very excited. I had come to grips with the fact that I was finally getting an opportunity to travel with the owner of my new company. He is the CEO. He is the Big Kahuna. With him as the president of the company, I seldom get an opportunity to have a one-on-one with this guy. I could feel my goose-bumps and I am truly looking forward to having both his listening ear and his direct input on this journey. I am in total disbelief that this type of chance has even opened up for me, let alone I was also getting an opportunity to take advantage of it. If only I could stop and pause for a moment, I'd ask myself the question, "Is this really happening to me?" There are a number of strategic "Gatekeepers" between him and me (bodyguards). That isn't necessarily bad. That is just the way it is.

I am what you call a licensed environmental instructor. On a regular basis, I teach lead-based paint classes, mold classes and asbestos classes. I teach locally and also throughout the US. This in turn has become my main source of income at the present time. On this particular day, the owner of my company and I are headed from Baltimore, Maryland to New York City to teach an Asbestos Awareness class to a client. Because I am fairly new to the company and its training department, the CEO, wanted to navigate and show me how things are done. Off-site clients are the exception and not the rule. To be singled out by him was special and my excitement surrounding this trip was more than just a passing fad. At this point in my employment, I believed I had done a pretty decent job. My instincts told me that having this time with the owner, while traveling up and back on the train, might give me a stronger insight as to what he thought of my progress in the company, up to now. I definitely wanted his opinion of my progress thus far. Off-line, he and I have had some very deep and intense conversations in the past about life. Many of those conversations were outside of the realm of business. On this occasion, I was hoping to get a gist or a temperature of where I stood within the company. Yet on this occasion, before we could get to exchange conversation about my concerns, something much heavier came to the surface and demanded our attention. It also started an intense, very thought provoking and gut-wrenching conversation. I had no idea at the time that this conversation would be the catalyst for compelling me to write several books. See, the conversation wasn't about me, my progress in the training department or about me as an employee. This conversation was so powerful that it compelled me to reflect on my seven years in upstate New York working with troubled inner-city, minority youth. Now that was all prior to me arriving at this company in Baltimore. So, my so-called preliminary employment evaluation has been put aside. This had now turned into a roller-coaster ride of my previous seven years in New York, changing the lives of misguided and impoverished kids - or so I thought. Or did I miss something?

**Political Correctness**

Since we live in an age where the moment you bring up politics, religion, race, sexual orientation/life-style, people automatically become defensive. I want to warn all of the readers before they get bogged down into reading this book that it has politics, sex, race, etc. But these items are not what the story is about, they are the tools or conveyances used to tell the story. I felt compelled to include this disclaimer based on what I see today in the exchange of conversations across this country. When did we become so polarized as a nation that if I don't agree with your point of view or ideas then we can't talk to one another like human beings? I hope that as these touchy issues arise in this story those who read it will be open enough to see beyond the surface of the items to see the impact on the overall story. These are real life issues and I'm telling them as they happened and were exposed.

**Who High-Jacked My Train?**

At Penn Station, the scheduled train was on time. We put our bags away and sat comfortably next to each other on the train, with the definite knowledge that this trip was probably going to take about two to three hours at least, one way. But before I go any further, I need to share some interesting information about the owner of my company and myself.

Let's call the owner Paul and my name is Jerome. Paul is in his forties and was brought up in and around Baltimore, Maryland. I would consider his journey poor to middle-class as compared to my up-bringing. He's married with children and spent some time serving his country in the United States Navy. He has also taken a small, thriving, up and coming engineering business and turned into a progressive, thriving and multi-layered, successful engineering organization. I would also have to say he has done well for himself and his family. Oh, and by the way, Paul is Caucasian.

As for myself, I'm in my fifties and I was also raised in Baltimore, Maryland, poor and from a family of eleven kids. I spent twenty-one years in the United States Army and I'm retired. I'm married with no children and spent seven years in New York State at a boot camp for delinquent youth before working at the engineering firm here in Baltimore. I am African-American.

Note, some might question the need or the validity for me to mention our race as I have shared our backgrounds, but race in this country touches a lot of areas and touches a lot of people. It is deeply rooted and very touchy. I believe both Paul and I are keenly aware of this fact. Nevertheless, I notice that neither of us have allowed it to be a factor in the progression of our professional and/or personal relationships. This unique paradigm for us has allowed our relationship to reach levels I had not anticipated. It has also reached levels that I see lacking in other relationships around me. And although I didn't allow race to keep me from being effective with the kids or my relationship with Paul, you will see how and where it shows itself throughout my story.

**No Filters Allowed**

As the train began to carry us in the direction of New York City, our conversation went from the very basic casual, to the very in-depth and penetrating. These types of conversations are not unusual for both Paul and me, but on this particular occasion, it became exceptional. To be candid, I knew Paul was good at probing, but I had no idea that his inquiry was going to take me to a place I hadn't been to in over two years; a place I had not planned to go to at all. It became very evident to me that in order to answer his question, I was going to be forced to go to a place that was uncomfortable, painful, yet quite exhilarating all at the same time. Paul is not only my employer, but a good friend. He possesses certain attributes and qualities that you only find in a few. For me, he has become an elevated person in my life with whom I don't have to filter my conversations before I share my thoughts or ideas. This is and has been a very unique position I have seldom found myself in, past or present. Most people I know and encounter require that in order for me to have an unfettered conversation with them, I must implement the appropriate filtering system to carry on a decent or profitable conversation with them. But, not so with Paul. You can only imagine how much I value and look forward to each opportunity to be in this type of situation with Paul. So, basically with Paul, I can let my hair down and let it rip. I can talk as much as I like, about anything that I like. Around him, I can be a straight shooter. And, when I get a chance, boy do we talk a lot.

# Chapter 2
# The Short Version

So, with no filtering allowed and no warning signs, Paul approached me with the following scenario. This African-American family from the inner-city of Baltimore has some smart kids. The kids' academics qualified them to go to a nearby Catholic school. The school was within walking distance from their house. The parents couldn't afford to pay for their tuition, so a donor stepped up and paid it for them. The school, in addition, has a dorm on campus for its distance and out-of-state students. Paul goes on to tell me that although this heaven-sent windfall enabled these kids to attend the school, them walking to and from school each day was causing a problem. As the Catholic students were taking their journey to and from school each day, they were being constantly bullied and harassed by other kids from the neighborhood. The students and the kids involved were not strangers. Each group knew each other. The parents, the school and the administrators, armed with this knowledge, tried to come up with a reasonable solution to this dilemma. With the help of a little research, it appeared this was only happening because these kids from the neighborhood were now going to this particular Catholic school and not a public school. The collective powers that be decided the appropriate solution and fix to this problem was as follows. Instead of allowing these students to walk each day to school, they would be housed on campus during the week and allowed to go home on the weekends. Although this solution eliminated the daily harassment of the students, it drove Paul out of his mind. Regardless of the fact that they did get to come home on weekends. I guess you could call the weekend visits some type of consolation? Yes? Paul distressfully commented about how sad this entire situation was for both the kids going to school, the kids harassing them and the overall impact on the home and the school. I could also see that Paul was totally frustrated and saddened that he couldn't find an answer to this unique quagmire. Since all the children of this story were African-American, I concluded that Paul trusted my insight and our unfiltered access with one another. This coupled with the fact that I am also African-American and grew up in Baltimore, Paul thought maybe I had an answer to the very question of Why?"

I said to Paul, "There is a long version of this story and there is a short version. Let me give you the short version first and then I'll give you the long one." The short version is "People do what they know." Most of those kids that lived in that neighborhood, probably couldn't pass the entrance exam to attend that Catholic school and definitely their parents couldn't afford to send them there, even if they could pass. So, for the kids who lived in this neighborhood to be attending this school and be Black also, put them on a higher level or status than the others who lived in that community. Under normal circumstances, to be receiving free tuition and access would be something to embrace, encourage and be celebrated; but, not so in this case. That is why the offensive response was directly associated with and to the attendees of the Catholic school. The mindset of some Blacks is that we are all in this together. Just because you have an opportunity to advance academically does not make you any better than us. There are those within the community who believe it is their appointed duty to ensure that the status quo is maintained and those who get a little bit extra don't forget where they originally came from. It doesn't matter how you got it or why. It needs to be addressed. It also needs to be attacked. It needs to be confronted in such a way so that those who benefit, don't forget that even if they go to the Catholic school they aren't any better than the rest of those who live there and go to regular public school. The harassment of these students was done in such a manner to ensure that the point is made very clear to them and any others who might attend this Catholic school as well. They better not forget where they came from or they were going to get the exact same type of treatment or even worse. For the kids doing the harassment, this wasn't personal or cavalier. It was a necessity.

This counter-productive, destructive behavior might seem strange to the average person. In some arenas, it is not even plausible, but not in the case where I come from. Some even call this "the crabs in a barrel mentality." In order for the crabs on the bottom to get out, they have to let the crabs on the top go first. Unfortunately, in this scenario, as those on the top attempt to try to exit, those on the bottom hold on to those on the top, and then nobody gets out of the barrel. It in turn becomes a lose-lose outcome for everyone.

To the average person, observing and listening to this scenario, it might appear strange, awkward, and even a little crazy; not to me. This type of behavior and outcome has been observed by me in the past and on different levels. It has been interwoven throughout my whole life. I am very familiar with the pain of this type of ugliness. Nevertheless, Paul stared at me in disbelief that such actions could and do exist. It was as if it didn't pass the common-sense test and it doesn't. But the reality is that this is a daily common occurrence, in the ghetto or where I come from. This type of insane treatment, unfortunately becomes the acceptable behavior and there seems to be no one who is willing to address it or even confront it for what it is. It almost becomes a norm. How sad. This type of thinking, where I come from, is not new. "Dog eat dog," is not the exception, it is the rule. You better watch your back or you better have your back watched. You're either invited to dinner or you are the dinner. The choice is yours. It all boils down to the way in which you carry yourself. Wow!

# Chapter 3
# Stuck Between The Short and Long Version

Since I have been a personal victim of this type of craziness for far too many times in my past, I then gave Paul a few personal examples about myself, along these other insights. I told him about two of my family members, on two different occasions who said the following to me, "You think you are better than the rest of the family, don't you?" Although my answer was no and it's been more than forty years since the incident, it still hurts today. I felt so betrayed and abandoned, but there was nothing I could do. My lack of self-worth had me crippled. I had to just accept what they said about me. Then I buried this traumatic experience as a teenager, the same way I tried to bury my experience with the kids in New York, when I felt compelled to depart. Yet, burying it didn't stop the pain. It only suppressed it. My short version to Paul was not sufficient. It didn't even scratch the surface.

I went on and felt compelled to open up and tell Paul about my upstate New York experience. Now, this was the long version. This is the version which very few people were aware of. Not even my family knew about this and what it entailed. I believed this would help give Paul some of the answers that he was desperately seeking. I honestly concluded that the short version was not enough. Now before I decide to step into this previous arena of my life, I knew that I had to come to grips with what I had personally and had deliberately buried for about two years. See up to now, I felt justified and satisfied that I had taken my New York State experience as a life lesson amongst others. What I had experienced there, I processed it and then buried it internally where I thought it rightfully belonged. I was even comfortable, based on my present employment and financial momentum that this past was not going to show its ugly face again. Boy, was I wrong. See, due to its complexity, I had packaged and processed it, then mentally and emotionally stored it so that I could then move on with the rest of my life without worrying about it. Up to this point, I was very pleased with this decision. To my astonishment, I realized I wasn't emotionally or spiritually prepared to go back to that place. See, I had done an extremely good job of providing a funeral and burial for that time of my life. But now, I am stuck in a quandary. Paul needed what I had buried, but I in-turn, was extremely comfortable with the fact that it was well hidden. I was now faced with a dichotomy. So, up to this point, there are no filters with Paul. But if I am going to keep it that way, I would have to raise the dead. If I changed and put up a filter, our relationship would never be the same.

Because I truly valued what Paul and I had and have been able to establish up to this point, I became keenly aware that I had absolutely no other choice in the matter. I knew what I needed to do. I knew what I had to do. If I was going to be honest, if I were going to truly be authentic, it became clear there were wounds I had carefully bandaged up and covered over that Paul's inquiry had begun to pull back the scabs on these wounds. I was in awe. At that very moment, I knew that I possessed exactly what my friend Paul was looking for. I needed to give him my long version. To have given him anything less, would have been a substitute. I also knew that in order to issue this proclamation, it was going to cost me a great deal. This moment reminded me of how exciting my time with those young men truly was. I was reminded of how I had reached the very essence of who I really was and had come to be as a leader, interacting with the kids.

Everything was coming full circle and to the forefront and in addition, to the good. I also remembered the bad and the ugly parts that should have never happened from the same people who said they cared about these kids (That's in Book 2). I was at a crossroad. I was in a quagmire. I was stuck. If I am going to help my friend Paul understand the rationale behind this dilemma of some Black kids going to school, then I had to go to a place that I thought was far behind me and that I had sufficiently buried. I had to confront an era that I believed was carefully tucked away inside of me and that I didn't need to worry about again or anymore. Well, guess what? I was stunningly misinformed. I was starting to think that this isn't fair. But who said life was fair? It was now or never.

# Chapter 4
# The Dirty Laundry, Please

I could definitely surmise from telling Paul some of these stories about myself that he could see how I could identify with the plight of those Catholic students who were just trying to get a decent education on the troubled streets of Baltimore. These kids needing to get to school every day and I had some things in common. I had personally been harassed during my K-12 years of school by kids who didn't want me to succeed either. It clearly appeared to me that Paul and I were in the same ballpark as it pertained to this matter of interference. In retrospect, Paul and I were also in agreement on a number of other levels as it pertained to life itself. Yet, there were still some unresolved issues that lingered in the untold atmosphere of life. What untold atmosphere you might ask? Paul couldn't ask me the questions, because I believe that he didn't know at the time what questions needed to be asked or even how to ask them. I also believed that I knew what the questions and the answers were, but here is my dilemma. Should I share it and/or will I share it? You see folks, there is an ugly term we use in our society as it pertains to us as groups/families/people. That term is called: "Dirty Laundry." Let's not get it twisted. There are a lot of things that you can tell or speak about, but you don't air your/our dirty laundry to anybody but family or to those of the inner-circle. It is an unwritten code. If you are rich, you share with the rich. If you are poor, you share with the poor. Blacks don't share with Whites and vice versa. There are just certain things that are kept to yourself or to your own people, period. Sounds to me like, I have a problem or do I?

As I was setting the previous stage of talking with Paul about my childhood, I was reminded of a few Whites who made a difference and had insight in my life. Then some others who were Black, had given up on me, completely. But not Mr. Posey, he was my 6th grade elementary teacher. I'll talk about him later. But he refused to give up on me. I'm now questioning whether or not I am going to give up on Paul. Since it falls in the category of dirty laundry, who is going to blame me? Mr. Posey didn't give up on me and I wasn't going to give up on Paul. I knew that I was not going to stop or hide. I also knew that I needed to take this soliloquy to the next level and that Paul was just the person to do it with. But what I didn't know was to what degree and how far I was willing to take it. I was at a crossroad. Paul had more than proven himself to be worthy of giving and receiving the dirty laundry trophy. Nevertheless, in some circles that is still not enough. There is also another side of this coin. Just because he is worthy, doesn't mean that he is ready. Another question that was running through my mind at this moment was, "Am I worthy or qualified to deliver this all-important message?" See, that's why they call it dirty laundry. It isn't just any laundry. Without the proper pre-treatment, washing and rinsing, the end product is much worse than the beginning. Although my credibility was intact, there was a part of this story that is still missing. There were some more pieces to this puzzle that I knew, but that I had yet to share with Paul. I can say with conviction and under normal circumstances, I would not have shared this information with Paul or even with other people in my inner circle. That's how deep it was. In retrospect, how many times in my past had I arrived at a moment like this? The answer is none. It was as if I were at a vortex in time that might never ever arise again. I also knew the decision to move forward rested solely on my shoulders. I knew this thing was deep. This thing was real deep.

So, as an African-American, I asked myself this thought-provoking question. "Is giving Paul what he is really looking for and in need of, a betrayal of that code of silence as it pertains to our people?" "Remember Jerome, too many others in the past who have done just that, actually, betrayed our people. Don't you be another one." Some may or may not believe this or accept this, at all. I also believe there are only a handful of Whites out there with whom I would have even considered sharing this type of conversation. Nevertheless, I had no trepidation about sharing this with my White friend, Paul. Since some who will read this book are going to accuse me of betrayal and being a sellout anyway, let me just get it out of the way right up front so I can move on. I hope and pray that as our society evolves to the point where more African-Americans will come to the realization that there is room at the Black table for some White folks. In addition, all White folks are not devils. All White folks are not the enemy. There is also an unwritten law which says that the opposite side will not understand, even if you share it with them. Guess what? That might be true, some of the time. That might be true, most of the time; but guess what? That is not true, all of the time. And to me and for me, my friend Paul is living proof of the fact that it is not true all of the time. I speak truth to life. I don't have to be conformed to what others think or say as it pertains to race. Race can only define me if I allow it too. I crossed that line and I crossed it boldly. I am not ashamed of it nor my friend. Paul has earned the right to hear my side of the story. He has earned the right to hear the African-American version. "How do you like me now?"

So, we have covered the short version of what took place on the crazy streets of Baltimore. We also looked at some of the reasons why and the possible alternatives to what actually brought it to past. I just gave Paul a little bit to nibble on. So, what about that long version? It's going to take more than just a few lines and a few paragraphs to explain the long version. On a previous trip taken by Paul and myself to Alabama, I told Paul that I thought he was an enigma. I told him that in all of my years of living on this earth, I have never met a White, Black or Hispanic man like him. He is truly, one of a kind. It seems that every time I was with him or around him, I was learning something about engineering, about people or about life. Paul was and is an amazingly, exceptional man. He told me that his mantra is, "I want to learn something new every day and I want to teach something new every day." So, at this crossroads, while sitting on this train, I became keenly aware that I had something that Paul needed and if I didn't give it up, we would both lose that day. Well, I don't consider myself a loser. Here goes.

### Where Is This Headed?

The setting for this long version takes place at a correctional facility in upstate New York. Nevertheless the answer that Paul is looking for has nothing to do with being incarcerated. Notwithstanding, I am using an incarcerated environment to give Paul what he truly needs to draw an appropriate conclusion. The journey that I was about to take Paul on was more than just a series of experiences, coupled with outcomes. I knew that I had to go in front of the camera, behind the camera and inside of the camera. Just telling the story alone was not enough. In addition, sharing the fact that most of the kids I released back into NYC were successful, wasn't enough either. I believed it was essential that I also included the issues and factors that led to this success. I took a seven-year journey at this facility. I was very successful at this facility. Nevertheless, I didn't truly realize my greatest accomplishments, until after I departed and resigned from that facility.

Let me get something straight. The most important piece of this story is hinged on my personal interaction with those young people and my ability to reach them where they were. Notwithstanding, there were other mitigating factors and issues that will not and cannot be ignored, because they make up the foundation on which this success could only be possible.

Up until now, all I've given to you is just a tease. It is nothing more than an appetizer. And now that I have your attention, I need to structure and set-up the table for your entrée. The chapters that follow will tell you a lot about these young people. They will also tell you a lot about me as the author. It will ultimately answer the question of "why and why not?" I take you back to the beginning and the ending. I show how one man can make a difference and leave a great legacy. I reveal how I not only saved them from the streets, but I saved them from themselves.

Paul just wanted something that worked. I knew in my heart that I couldn't just give him what he asked for. It became very clear to me that in order to give him what he needed, I had to go deeper than I had planned to. I also knew that it was going to cost me something. I knew there was a price to be paid. Things that are worthwhile, don't come cheap. "What's in your wallet?"

# Chapter 5
# Before I Could Tell Their Story, I Had To Tell His-Story

As I anxiously began to tell their story, it became very obvious to me that another story had to be told, first. And it had to be told before I could tell the story about the kids. I needed to tell my story. Initially, my focus was strictly on the kids and their experiences. I purposely wanted as little of my story told as possible, because this journey wasn't about me, but about them. As well-meaning as my intentions were, I quickly became aware that their story was not going to be enough when it came to the issue of credibility; my credibility. History played a role. But it was not the primary role. Since I was just another adult in their everyday lives, what made me stand apart? Why did I stand out and what made me any different than those other adults at this facility? That's when I knew that I had to tell His-story, with their story. Far too many of these young men reminded me of who I was and where I had come from. I realized that I or anyone who was going to embrace the lives of these kids', needed to know what gave us the audacity to even attempt to convey our experience while trying to impact their experience. Interesting enough, once I had shared my story with them, telling their story became so much easier. My story is not a story of fiction. It is the truth, the whole truth and nothing but the truth. If you have lived it, then you can tell it. And boy, did I live it.

To the parents, teachers, adults, counselors and care-givers, I would like to share one more thing. I hope and pray that as you read my story it will help you find, your story. In addition, I hope you will keep your story in mind as you read and walk through this book. I believe that who you are and where you come from, will influence what you send forth. Knowing one's self, what triggers you and what you will or will not accept, will also determine your effectiveness on others and the kids. When I was forced to reflect on my own story, I quickly realized why I had success after success with the kids. I also realized why telling their story wasn't at all complicated or troubling. I welcomed being their spokesperson and embraced telling their truth. For their truth is my truth. The Good Book said, "The truth shall make you free." Not set you free, it will make you free.

(**NOTE**: *I also talk more about my personal truth in Book 2.*)

I grew up in an all-Black neighborhood in Baltimore City and I attended an all-Black elementary school. As I was transitioning into junior high school, the Black kids in the elementary school told me horror stories about what to expect from the White kids once I got into the seventh grade. Having no form of reference to compare their allegations to or anyone to go to and verify the validity of these comments, I found out later that most of what was conveyed to me was either a lie or just hearsay. It appears that none of what I was told, was founded in truth. I'm so glad that I didn't accept their words just because the kids were Black. The irony of the whole matter was the same things the Blacks told to me about what to expect from the Whites is exactly how the Blacks eventually treated me. I was so saddened and disappointed by this revelation. Yet, something inside of me would not allow me to accept those lies nor to perpetuate them on the intended target (Whites) nor turn on those who tried to deceive me (Blacks). Sadly enough, too many of them were deceived as well and were only passing on the same mess that they were told. Sadly, this vicious type of cycle is so prevalent, even in today's society. We call t bullying and racism.

    When I reached the ninth grade, things at home were much different than in previous school years. By the time I reached high school, I wanted a lot more than what life had handed me when I was in elementary and middle school. I spoke about this earlier as it pertained to two people in my family. This hunger played out when two of my family members (at different times), looked me in the eye and said, "You think you're better than the rest of this family, don't you?" Although my answer was no, it couldn't remove the sting of the knife that had been plunged deep into my heart by the nature of their comments. The tears swelled up within my eyes in total disbelief to hear these words more than once. When I should be looking to them for love, direction, and guidance for my future, I am now being told by the same people that I am stuck up and think I am better than they are. See, I didn't know that there were classifications of the poor, within the poor. I thought poor was poor. Had I convinced them or had they convinced themselves that there were different degrees of poor? I did try to convey to them verbally that I didn't think that I was any better than they were, but that I did deserve to want to be somebody in life. I didn't want to end up as a statistic. Can somebody please tell me, how in the name of the God of heaven, could they have believed this of me? Yet in retrospect, if I could name one thing or one person that influenced me to the point where I might be giving off this type of vibe to others, I would have to put the blame squarely on the shoulders of one sixth-grade teacher, Mr. Posey. I have to also say that he was more than just a mere teacher. His impact and influence over me, literally changed my life and my future; but at that time, I had no clue how much. It was Mr. Posey's impression and impact that gave me the greatest success while I was working with those underprivileged and misguided kids, and I will forever be grateful to him as a result of it.

# Chapter 6
# The 6th Grade Teacher Who Changed My Life

From my heart to the universe, Mr. Posey is one of those once in a lifetime people that if you are fortunate enough to meet or run into, you should count yourself blessed. Before I tell you how he impacted my life, let me tell just a little about this abnormal, larger-than-life, man. He made it a point to show you how to present and carry yourself in public. He gave respect and he demanded respect. Although at times he seemed overwhelming, he really cared about kids. He stood about 6'4", and weighed about 240 pounds. He seemed like a giant; but a gentle giant. He not only taught us academics, he also taught us about life and life skills. He didn't make excuses and he didn't accept excuses. He made sure that we were informed about the importance of personal hygiene and cleanliness. He showed us how to carry ourselves as proud men and women. You had to be prepared when you came into his class, because you didn't know when you were going to be called upon. You had to bring your "A" game to class or you were in trouble. Mr. Posey embarrassed a lot of students during the school year. I was one of them. But that embarrassment was always to make you a better student and a better person. It was never ever used to belittle or to degrade you.

Everybody, including the parents, the students and his fellow teachers highly respected Mr. Posey. I remember on one occasion, it was time to teach sex-education to us in the sixth-grade, but the school needed permission from the parents before it could be taught. My parents said no. Mr. Posey invited both my parents to the school and they met with him and the principal. When my parents emerged from that meeting, my Dad told me that I would be having sex-education with Mr. Posey. Although, I never asked why. I was completely dumb-founded. When my parents said no, they didn't change their minds. How in the world did Mr. Posey and the principal get them to say yes? Wow! This was unbelievable.

Before attending Mr. Posey's class, my personal expectations and my individual drive for life were very low and that was just fine by me. Since I didn't expect much, I didn't look for much either. There is a saying, "Nothing ventured; nothing gained." I felt content and very satisfied with my status in life and that was enough for me. Now, Mr. Posey on the other hand, set the bar extremely high and expected you to at least reach for the bar, if nothing else. He created an atmosphere that either brought out the best in you or the worse in you. Oh, and by the way, it didn't matter to Mr. Posey which avenue you chose. He wasn't going to change, period. He didn't have to change. He knew exactly who he was. You see, I wasn't a great student. I was just a decent, average student back then. When I finished my given assignments in class, I would sit quietly and wait for further instructions. Mr. Posey also noticed this pattern of behavior and noticed in most cases that I was not a disruptive student. I would just sit there quietly. One day he asked me why was I just sitting there doing nothing and not working on the math assignment he had just given us. I replied that I was finished. When he came over and checked my work, it became evident that I was right on the money with the lessons he taught and had a very good grasp of the concepts presented. Then he did something that caught me totally off guard and left me completely puzzled. He instructed me to help my fellow student sitting nearby with her work. I was so taken aback by this that I almost fell out of my chair. I then internally questioned his motives and his sincerity. I said within myself, "Is this a set-up? He can't be talking to me. You want me to help another student? Me? You mean to tell me that I not only have value, but it is good enough to be given or passed on to another human being?" Of course, the answer to all of these questions was yes, but not to me. This can't be happening to me, above all the students present, Mr. Posey had obviously lost his ever-loving mind. He must have me mixed up with some other student in the classroom. Up until this time, I constantly questioned my very validity, my purpose and my own self-worth. While I was trying to figure out who I was, Mr. Posey went a step further and just pulled the rug right out from underneath me with this scenario. So, as he requested, I quietly went on and helped the young lady sitting next to me with her math and she began to understand. This experiment of his paid off hefty dividends to all who were involved, including myself. I was dazed, confused and exhilarated all at the same time. For me, I had just achieved the impossible. While in total disbelief, he then went on to tell me something that would change my life forever. He said, "Jerome, you can be anything you want to be in life, if you just put your mind to it." These were strange, foreign and unfamiliar proclamations for me. I was so used to hearing the negative, I knew that Mr. Posey must have been mistaken with this assessment. How could I possibly possess the attributes that he was describing? There must be some type of flaw in his internal compass. I can't be that person that he is talking about. Nevertheless, throughout the school year, Mr. Posey called upon me to assist other classmates who needed help. I have to give Mr. Posey his props. He knew something that I didn't know and he knew that it was going to take more than just conversation for me to obtain it. He didn't just tell me of my worth, he showed and demonstrated to me with irrefutable evidence every day, contrary to my stinking-thinking, that I had worth. He placed me in a position in which I could not deny, refute, explain or even understand what was happening to me. I had taken his instructions during class, understood them for myself and was then able to convey that same information to another student who was struggling. Mr. Posey explained that he, the struggling student and myself all benefited from this experience. He conveyed that by spending less time with that particular student, it in turn, gave him more time to reach and teach more information to more students, including me. Mr. Posey, through this process had inadvertently conveyed to me that I had true worth and that I really counted for something. At the same time that all of this was unfolding, I was having a serious mental struggle just grasping all of this. Then it hit me like a ton of bricks. Somebody truly needed what I (Jerome) had to offer and what I had to offer was mine and mine alone. I had created it. Everybody else didn't have what I had to offer. Since the evidence he had presented to me was undeniable, I had no other choice but to believe him and accept it. At this point, the affirmation, "I am somebody," is now more than just a catch phrase spoken to me from the teacher. I am now positioned in a place in life that I had never experienced before and it felt good. It felt really good. Thank you, Mr. Posey.

To think that up to this point in my life, I was very content with the phrase "going along, to get along." It fit me to a tee. I chose to maintain the status quo and stay in my lane. Yet as a direct result of Mr. Posey interrupting my life, I realized that the apple cart had been overturned and I knew that I could no longer accept things just on face value or just because somebody else said it. I can think for myself. I can have an opinion and I can share it if I choose to. I have true value and it is worth something. This for me was a game changer. Did everything in my life start to change after this transformation? No. Did I now have it all figured out to where I was going and how I was going to get there? Absolutely not? But I will tell you this. It is one of the earliest points in my life where I knew failure did not have to be the only option I had to choose from. This new knowledge for me was priceless!

So up until the introduction of Mr. Posey in my life, I was doing what I knew. I was doing what was comfortable. I was doing what came naturally. I was doing what others were doing. I had become complacent and content. I was even happy, if I really think about it. With no goals or anything to shoot for, I was okay. Internally, as I thought about the story my friend Paul shared with me when we were on the train to New York, I knew I could have been the student chosen to go to the Catholic school or one of those kids who harassed those who had been chosen to go. For me, Mr. Posey stopped this vicious cycle. I not only started looking at others differently, I began to look at myself differently. When I looked, I didn't always like what I saw, but I then had some tools by which to deal with it. Up until that point, I was just lost and didn't even know it. Armed with these tools, I could see why certain family members thought I was a turn-coat or stuck-up. It's just that I didn't know how much I had and I was changing to the point where others thought I was just out there. I also realized that I wasn't mature enough at the time to put all of this together. Nevertheless, it was still very painful the way my own family spoke to and treated me. Being that I was younger than them, I couldn't help but expect a little more from them. But guess what? I realized later that it really wasn't their fault. They didn't have it within them to give to me and if I had asked for it, they couldn't give it even if they wanted to. You can't give, what you don't have. Interesting!

What was truly amazing about what took place between Mr. Posey and myself was that this was nothing less than a miracle. You see, I thought everybody had a Mr. Posey in their lives to help them in school and to help them along the way. I didn't learn until later that Mr. Posey was truly the exception and not the rule. So why me; why was I singled out for such an amazing awakening? Good question, I'm still looking for the answer to that elusive selection process. You see, I consider myself just an everyday, ordinary guy.

I believe the sharing of these personal experiences about Mr. Posey with Paul set the stage for what I was about to drop on him, and I knew that he didn't have a clue as to what was coming from me. Nevertheless, I also didn't have a clue that I would ever be sharing this information with him or with any White person on such a personal and intimate basis. Yet in retrospect, I am so glad that I did.

So, before I start on the rest of this journey, before I start conveying the rest of the story, I am compelled to stop and say "Thank you," to Paul personally. I know I told him thank you in person, but I felt compelled to put in writing as well. Thanks again Paul.

In conjunction with the story I told you about Mr. Posey, after I retired from the United States Army and returned to Baltimore, Maryland, I found Mr. Posey's phone number in the phone book. I called him and thanked him for changing my life forever. We had a wonderful conversation and he did remember me. That was truly an amazing experience.

# Chapter 7
# My Journey Beyond The Brokenness

On the surface, what took place with Mr. Posey and me, might not appear important to the average person. Notwithstanding, it was very important to me. Mr. Posey and I were not just a teacher and student whose pathways crossed. I believe that Mr. Posey sparked a fire within me that I was unaware even existed. Mr. Posey left his mark on me and at the time, I didn't have a clue. What he did was pivotal in placing me on a journey that not only impacted me, but mankind. Below are some of the encounters which occurred along the way that convinced me I was not just another person moving through life. I was on a mission and not the kind of mission that most people get to take. As life's journey moved me, I repeatedly found myself either helping with young people or teaching students. It became an interesting turn of events. I also came to realize I was pretty good at it.

**Being A Teacher's Aide At Another School**

After I departed the 6th grade and moved on, I became aware that my confidence was somewhat stronger and somewhat bolder. While in the 9th grade, there was a request for students who wouldn't mind being student aides at a local elementary school. I volunteered. What I learned later was that this particular school was short of both teachers and aides, and the school board had given them permission to seek the nearby high school students to help out. All volunteers had to be in good standing and recommended by a teacher in their own school. I jumped at this opportunity and had a wonderful time assisting with a 3rd-grade class. I knew this was a special opportunity and not everyone would be allowed to participate. But, I got to be a part of it. I was all up in the midst of it and was loving making a difference. I was a reflection of what Mr. Posey started back in the sixth-grade and I truly enjoyed paying it forward.

**Working With Those At-Risk, Before The Age Of 20**

While at my first duty station (Fort Hood Texas) in the Army, I volunteered as a house parent at a residential corrections facility in Central Texas. The facility was short of personnel and I thought I could be of service. Even though I had never worked in this type of environment before, I wanted to make a difference with these troubled youth. I distinctly remember one of the kids who was trying to ultimately play me. He was talking to another kid, but he wanted to make sure I could clearly hear him. He was telling this other kid that he was going to escape and get out of this place. Since I believed that his statement was spoken for my benefit, I didn't challenge his convictions, but I did challenge his rationale. After he confirmed to me that I heard him correctly, I asked him what is your game plan? He looked somewhat puzzled. I believe this was because he wasn't expecting that question. I then began to share with him some of the obvious obstacles and barriers that he would have to face and navigate, just in the local community alone, to achieve this. Knowing I had his attention, I broadened the scope of items he needed to have and should take under consideration, if he was truly serious about such an undertaking. When I got through talking to him and the others who were present, all of the wind had gone out of his sails. The look on his face with his mouth closed, was priceless. I didn't tell him he was wrong, I just showed him some missing pieces to his thought process. I then told him that it isn't that you planned to fail, you failed to plan. When I exited the facility later that day there was a strong feeling of accomplishment as it pertained to how I had handled the situation and dealt with that young man. Only a few kids and myself knew what had taken place during this encounter, but it was powerful. Every time I returned to that facility, this young man was all over me because of what I said to him the first time we met. He knew I was the real deal and not like the other adults. Imagine how that made me feel? Imagine what that did for my ego?

## Working With All Females

A few years later, I found myself stationed at Fort Stewart, Georgia, as an assistant coach of an all-girls softball team. The young woman who brought me on board thought these girls needed a man's touch. And she was right. As I watched the girls in practice, I just hung my head. They were terrible. I had to be honest with them. I told them that if they wanted to win, they needed to play like boys and not girls. I told these young ladies that when the ball was hit at them, they had to get in front of it. Bend and close their legs. By doing this, even if they didn't catch it, the ball wouldn't get by them. I told them they couldn't be afraid of the ball. They had to attack it when it left the bat. This was the pep talk that I would give these girls on a daily basis. They started doing exactly what I told them. Guess what? They started winning games instead of losing. I was oh, so proud of that intervention. What was interesting was the fact that I didn't know how to teach them how to play like girls and win. I only knew how to teach them how to play like boys, but it worked. And everybody was happy.

## Touching The Asian Nation Of Korea

Next the Army deployed me to South Korea. While stationed at Camp Humphrey, I heard of an orphanage in the local village. My visits to this place became one of the highlights of my overseas tour. This wasn't just any orphanage. It was filled with mainly children of

American and Asian descent. These are bi-racial children or as what some unfortunately called them, half-breeds. Their fathers were American and their mothers were Korean. Many of these babies ended up in this place because nobody wanted them. They were considered throw-a-ways. They were rejects. I distinctly remember an incident on one of my visits, sitting with one of these young ones. She allowed me to pick her up, but she was looking at me strangely. She then began to rub my face as if it was dirty. I then rubbed my face real hard and said to her that it doesn't rub off. This is me. This is all of me. I then hugged her real tight. She wasn't being offensive. She had never seen an African-American before. I thought this was a beautiful cultural exchange that would have never happened, if I had stayed on base and decided not to venture out and experience the culture of a foreign land.

**Next Stop Germany**

My next big encounter with young people came when the Army stationed me in Germany. During this time, the military was downsizing in Europe at a number of its military bases. They were closing bases and civilian personnel and military families were mostly being returned to the US. Because of my job title, Personnel Sergeant, I was greatly needed to help with this large transition. After my fourth move in the country, I found myself at the small base teaching the Sunday School class to the local teenagers. I loved it. I also discovered there was a group called Club Beyond that worked with teenagers who lived on the base and those from the local community. This Club Beyond was an extension of Youth-For-Christ, a program for military kids. Club Beyond reached out and evangelized the young people. Since some of the kids in my Sunday School class were also in Club Beyond, I found out the group needed volunteers, so I stepped up. I had no clue what I was about to get involved in. I thought that I was just volunteering to help-out with the kids. Wrong. We supervised games, outings, camping, Bible study and recruiting other youth to the club. We even went to Nairobi, Kenya for three weeks to help build a playground at a local school. The experience with Club Beyond and the kids was amazing. I talked. I listened. I cried with and cried for these young people. I even watched some of them get saved. You could not stand on the sidelines as an observer and still somehow be involved with this organization. It would suck you right in. There was a strong need of belonging and I was there to assist with helping them fit in. I truly had the time of my life watching the transformation of these kids, but also the transformation of myself. Not only did I help these kids find themselves, I was good at it. I was very good at it. Amazingly, I didn't know how good I was until I stepped out on faith to make a difference. That was all it took. This only happened because there was a need and I decided to volunteer, period. See, I am a firm believer that nothing beats a failure, like a try. That was all I did. I tried and I succeeded.

**Then Nairobi, Kenya**

As mentioned, my tour in Germany and working with Club Beyond, opened up an opportunity for me to visit Nairobi, Kenya. Our main objective was to build a playground at a local school, do some sight-seeing and go on a Safari. As a foreigner, I knew that we would mostly be isolated while visiting Kenya. We would spend most of our time at the school working on the playground. My first day in-country set the tone for this entire miraculous trip. Upon our arrival to Nairobi, they allowed us to spend a couple of hours in the local village to do some shopping and sightseeing. I personally didn't buy anything, but I did have what I thought was a beautiful experience, until I was told later that I was in grave danger. I was sharing with my fellow-travelers how I met this group of boys, which ranged from the ages of about 8-14 and there were about 8 of them together in an isolated area. I stopped and began to engage them in conversation and they in turn, politely returned my inquiries. It appears that the leader's name was Abraham. Somewhat puzzled that this group of boys was on the street at this time of day and not in school, I asked Abraham, "Isn't this a school day?" He replied, yes. My next question was then why aren't you guys in school? Abraham replied that school cost money and their parents didn't have any money to send them to school. I responded, so you guys are just hanging out? They replied yes. I then said, I don't know about Kenya, but in America, when young boys have nothing to do, they usually get in trouble. The laughter and chuckling I heard confirmed that the same applies in Kenya. I was utterly fascinated and not startled. I received a very positive vibe from these boys and from Abraham. I then called Abraham out from the group and spoke to him about 5 feet away from everyone else. As I spoke to Abraham, I also had my back to the group so the rest of them couldn't see or hear the exchange with Abraham. I then opened my fanny-pack and pulled out some US money and Kenyan shillings and gave them to Abraham. I told him that it was for him and the others. I told him that since he knew who needed what to make sure they got it. He put the money away. I turned back to the group and said good-bye and thanked them for a wonderful time. I then returned to our bus and group.

Later that night, as I was sharing this encounter with one of my fellow-travelers, It was obvious that I was excited and blown away about what had taken place with these kids. A young man from the camp, William interjected and said that you don't know how lucky you are. I was puzzled. He said, that those type of kids are always targeting the tourists and robbing them. It's a wonder they didn't gang up on you, take your fanny-pack and hurt you. Now, don't get me wrong, I understood his concerns, but I don't think he really got the gist of the whole story. I believed that in and of itself, this was not a chance encounter. I believed it was divine intervention and was meant to be. Not once did I feel any danger or a threat from these boys. Remember, I'm from the streets of Baltimore. We don't play. You've got to be on point and have your wits about you at all times to survive on our streets. I didn't leave those wits at home. I brought them to Nairobi with me. If I hadn't I would have been an accident, just waiting to happen. I don't bel eve I was a target, because I didn't carry myself as a target. I believe that there was mutual respect. When there is mutual respect, there is dialogue. Those kids enjoyed my company and I enjoyed theirs. There was a connection and a positive exchange. Notwithstanding, I didn't know how true this mutual respect would be until I was about to depart and head back to Germany from Kenya.

On the day that I ran into Abraham again, it was only a few days before I departed Nairobi. William, one of the missionaries from camp we stayed at, dropped me off at the local college, while he went into town and picked up supplies for the camp. I met with my friend and his wife, whom I hadn't seen for years. I met them before in the US and they had later returned home to Kenya. Upon William's return to pick me up, we stopped back in the local town, so I could get lunch. While we were walking in the town, I got to talk with William about himself and his goals for the future. He made it clear that he wanted to reach out and minister especially to those lost kids that everyone had given up on. While this conversation was taking place, guess who we ran into, Abraham, again? One of those lost kids. Two other kids were with him. I believed our meeting was divinely staged. I introduced Abraham and William to one another. I asked Abraham how he was doing and was there anything that I could do for him. He said that he was fine, but he stated that he was hungry. Then William and I proceeded to enter a grocery store. I purchased a loaf of bread and 3 packs of meat. I stood there in the store and made the sandwiches and placed them inside the bread bag. When William and I returned to the spot where Abraham stood, it went from three people, to about thirty young men. I quickly recognized my dilemma. I didn't have enough sandwiches for thirty people and this could be problematic. I immediately turned to Abraham and said, you know who is most deserving. You tell me who to feed. Abraham, orderly pointed out each child to receive a sandwich. When I got to the last sandwich, I gave it to Abraham. Everyone then dispersed peacefully. I shared with William the lesson I believe God was trying to teach us. I am leaving to return to America, but he will still be here to witness to these kids. I gave them physical food. When he gets a chance to approach them, they will remember that he was with the Black man from America who give them physical food, but now God has opened the door for him to give them spiritual food. What an amazing blessing and miracle that will be. I thought I was just coming to Kenya to build a playground. This encounter with William, Abraham and these kids, was just the tip of the ice-berg. I was left speechless.

# Chapter 8
# The Long Version Set-Up

From being a teacher's aide in the ninth grade, to going to Kenya from Germany, I had no clue how all of these encounters were to prepare me for after retirement. All I knew was that I was good with kids, period. For me to take you from the short version to the long version, we need to take an unusual route I am next about to take you on a journey with kids from a correctional facility. That's right, a correctional facility. Previously, I took you on a territorial journey to different places and with different children whom I have encountered locally and all over the world. I even took you on a journey through my childhood and you met my 6th grade teacher, Mr. Posey. This happened, long before I ended up at this facility, I was on a path to reach kids and especially those kids who were in trouble or needed help. I was like a magnet. Over and over, I was drawn to the needy and the needy were drawn to me. It is clearer for me to see now that I was positioned for success then and I didn't even have a clue. Don't get me wrong. I am not complaining. It's just that I didn't connect the dots until now. Before I could take Paul there and before I take you on the long version, there are a few more things that I need to explain first I'm going to be telling you a story about a correctional-facility that I worked at in upstate

New York, a few years back. On the surface, it might not appear to fit in with the past choices I made, but it does. I need you to be patient with me and give me just a little more lee-way. I plan to show you just how brokenness fits into the long version. I will share with you a story that will absolutely blow your mind. I didn't plan for this opportunity nor did I plan to situate myself in a position to end up working at this facility. Initially, it was just another job and maybe a chance to give back. But in turn, I found out later that I would be working with some at-risk youth just like I'd grown up with and had previously worked with. I had no idea or inkling as to what I had gotten myself into or where it was going to take me. And by the time I began to figure things out, it was already too late. I had been sucked in and hooked.

Ending up at a correctional facility after retirement, on the surface, might seem strange. It was not my first choice. I feel a compelling need to give you at least a little background information about taking this job. I needed to pose or should I say, expose a few objectives about my choice. In my past, I have been involved in classroom settings, a youth group at church, a daycare center and even involved in a neighborhood youth group setting. What and how would this journey be of any benefit to me or you? If you had asked me this same question some fifteen-years ago when I first started writing this book, I might have said, very little. But, I now sincerely believe that I would have been wrong, very wrong. I believe that the principles and concepts laid out in books 1 & 2 of Fixing The Broken, Without Being Broken, are universal principles. These principles are based on my examples and exchanges through life. If you were to say there is room for additional stories and examples, I would have to agree with you 100%. Nevertheless, these events and experiences are autobiographical. They are not one size fits all. And, they are not hypothetical. Each example that I share and explain, I experienced personally. No embellishments or extras. What I share is exactly what happened on the ground. Each person and each experience can and could have turned out totally different in another time and in another space, but these are my examples. These are my experiences. Since a lot of what happened was successful, I thought this would be a very good place to start and shine some light on the importance of keeping it real. This was truly the place which afforded me the ability to turn on the light switch, so that those exposed could see what was missing and what was really in-place. Some might even call it a game-changer. I would like to say that this particular environment allowed those who chose to participate a chance to clearly see the missing pieces or to see what those other pieces really resembled. See, once all of the pieces are together, you can get the job done. You can complete the puzzle.

Since I've already given you the short-version, my credentials and a little bit about my background, I thought I would do the same as it pertains to how I got to this facility and how it became the perfect vehicle for me to extract, the long version. You see, I was just looking for a job after I retired. I want to make that perfectly clear from the out-set. It was not necessarily my intention to fix the broken, per-se or try to save the world. I kind of got drafted, but I liked it. So, I decided to give it a try. Oh, by the way, if you happen to respect my advice and believe I have some credibility, let me share something else with you, don't do this on the fly. This is really hard work, if you care. In addition, it can also destroy you, if you are not prepared. I wanted to quit, more than once. By the time those hooks had penetrated my self-worth, my self-esteem and my soul, it was already too late for me. I was like Chuck. I was already stuck and there was no turning back. My goal was to size it all up. I planned to hit my side, your side and the side that neither of us was aware of. This was not a game.

Once I take you through the background of the facility and how I ended up being there, I plan to take you into some of the one-on-one settings between myself and the kids. I'm also going to hit you with some group settings. Those tend to get very interesting. I will not nor do I plan to take you on every ride at the amusement park. I have selected certain episodes that I deem critical to my experience and to the overall outcome. I also tried to step into their shoes so as to not forget how it was when I was growing up. I came to realize that there was very little difference between them and me. When it is all said and done, I will expose you to the good, the bad and the ugly. I wouldn't have it any other way. You will see that any of my successes or breakthroughs were based on a little give and take. They are not based on scripts, a set of rules or any particular precedent. Scripts and rules are nothing more than outlines. It takes a cooperative, to produce positive results. And, last but never least, you can't fake it, till you make it. The truth will come out, and it always rises to the surface. It will expose any fallacies and/or deceptions. The truth also will not discriminate. It doesn't matter who you are or what you are. It will inevitably expose you. And, let me tell you something else about this exposure, it can be real ugly and It doesn't care who you are. Note: Speaking of ugly, I saved most of the real ugly for Book 2. I did that because most of the ugly wasn't about the kids. Besides, I'm trying to stay on point. Some of you are only interested in the basics and how it can help you in most situations. Nevertheless, there are those times when you have got to go below the surface. When that happens, sometimes it gets ugly. Sometimes, it gets real ugly. But are you ready? Oh by the way, those ugly times are what truly spawned me to write Book 2. Hello!

# Chapter 9
# You Can't Function Without Properly Calibrating Your GPS. Was It Six-Figures Or Go Figure

As I began to give Paul the explanation of the long version to his earlier questions, I knew I was also going to have to tell him why I voluntarily walked away from the last job I had in New York and later came to work for his company. Up until now, I basically told him that it was just time for me to move on, so I did. Well, there was a little more to the story than that. When I put in my resignation at my last job, it had gotten to the point where I felt like I was a one-legged man in a butt-kicking contest. There was just no way I could win at it, any more. Before I knew it, my successes were actually getting the kids in trouble. That is when I knew it was time to call it quits. In order for me to tell this story, I need to first set the groundwork about my last job, so everyone can understand why this job played such a pivotal role in not only shaping these kids' lives, but the lives of others and even my life.

In upstate New York, there are several training facilities for youth. I worked at a boot-camp style facility, geared specifically for boys between the ages of 12-18. I worked at this facility for approximately seven years. So many of these boys mimic and emulate the same behaviors Paul spoke about in this initial story. The only difference is, these boys are at this facility in most cases as a direct result of a judge passing sentence on that same type of criminal behavior. In other words, these kids were locked up. Point blank, they were in jail. In addition, the majority of these kids were minorities. When I came on board and took the job at this facility, I was under the belief that I could really make a difference with these kids. What I didn't know was that, I would one day end up being much like a Mr. Posey with these kids. That was not my initial goal at the out-set of this employment opportunity. But, I am in no way complaining that it eventually turned out that way. As I think back on it at the time, I believed I acquired this position strictly by default. Or was it by divine intervention? You tell me.

After completing seven successful years at this place, I walked away from the facility in emotional tears. I carried a distinct feeling that I had done the best job I could, but I also carried a weight upon my departure that I was leaving with the job, not yet quite finished. Fortunately, I later learned that I was very mistaken. I left exactly when I needed to leave. I also accomplished exactly what I needed to accomplish, and it was definitely time to move on. And, to think that I was initially headed to Atlanta to start making six-figures a year, but was delayed, seven of those years. Hummm!

Before I share with you what I conveyed to Paul about the rest of the story, I believe it is imperative that I set the stage and groundwork for the inquiring minds who are wondering about how in the world I got to the point where I could even tell this story. Due to the bond and trust that Paul and I have, I didn't need to go into a lot of details about the facility, how I got there, or even why I stayed. Neither did I have to tell Paul why I was compelled to leave when I did leave. Nevertheless, for those in my audience, I will set the stage for this story and why I need to tell it in the first place.

**Atlanta Here I Come**

Some will call it weird, while others will call it destiny. Some might even call it perfect timing. After faithfully serving twenty-one years on active duty in the United State Army, I was determined to retire in Atlanta, Georgia, find me a six-figure a year job, and enjoy the rest of my life in the South. Considering these lofty goals, I hadn't done too badly. But at the time of the writing of this book, I was still looking for that six-figure job and I only had one chance to visit the city of Atlanta, since my retirement in 1996.

So instead of six-figures, how in the world did I ever get put into the position to make a difference and impact the lives of minority teenagers? Good question. Well, my twenty-one years of active-duty military service was coming to an abrupt close. All of my reliable research told me that the best place for me to retire was in Atlanta, Georgia. So, I decided to follow the money. In addition, part of my military out-processing included job searching opportunities. While preparing for departure and travel, I was also preparing for employment. I knew that my resume, references and my contacts were going to play a major role as I moved forward. I was ready for anything or anybody, so I thought.

Having been raised in Baltimore, Maryland and now retiring out of the Fort Drum, New York arena, the question was raised more than once as to why I was headed to Atlanta and not back to Baltimore City. To be honest, I'm still looking for that answer as well. I own a house in Baltimore, and most of my wife's and my family live in Baltimore. Both my wife and I were born and raised in Baltimore. I have a lot of networking contacts in Baltimore. Yet, ultimately for me, it was just another, faith walk. All of my research in the library and on the Internet said that Atlanta was the place to settle in for "My Retirement." It was the best place to settle my family and myself. So, Atlanta here I come. Not.

My initial goal was to leave my wife in the Baltimore area with her family and then travel to Atlanta first. Upon my arrival in Atlanta, I would stay at Fort McPherson, Georgia until I could find a one-bedroom apartment for us. Next, I would crank up the job hunting.

Once housing and employment were in place, I would then head back to Baltimore and get my wife for the return trip. This MO (Modus Operandi) is nothing new. My wife and I used this method of relocation during our reassignments for my last eighteen years of service in the Army, and it worked beautifully. We never lost money on any assignment or reassignment while in the Army.

But, needless to say, I never made it to Atlanta. Neither did I make it to Baltimore right after my retirement. I ended up in a really small town in upstate New York, working part-time for the State of New York and hoping they would later bring me on as a permanent employee. In those years of military moves with my wife, we never lost a dime, when we moved from base to base. Yet, by the time I moved to Central New York to take the job, I was more than twenty-five thousand dollars in credit card debit, and I didn't know from week-to-week whether I would be called into work or not. I didn't know how nor did I have the means to procure enough money to pay all of my monthly bills. News flash; "Jerome, you're in big trouble."

Something Doesn't Add Up

How did things get so bad, so crazy, so quickly? Another good question. There I was at age forty, about to embark upon my second career in life. Most people are lucky if they have one career. My plans were all laid out and I was ready to execute them. Atlanta here I come, remember. But, there was only one problem. A good friend of mine, who knew that I enjoyed working with kids and was good at it, told me about this correctional facility in upstate New York that was looking for staff. She explained how these kids were all inner-city youth who were locked up, and came from the same type of place that I came from growing up in Baltimore. She explained how this six-month program was sending them back to the streets of New York City with a chance to turn their lives around. Now as much as I believed in it, I figured If I spend the next two years in Atlanta, I would be making at least six figures a year. Now here is what was interesting. That money possibility alone didn't excite me as much as the possibility of turning those young men's lives around. I knew within me that I could make six-figures a year, anywhere. But, what about the chance to work with and affect the lives of these at-risk youth. I told myself, these are the same kids you grew up with, Jerome. And, where are most of them now? They aren't retired and they aren't making six-figures. I could not escape these facts. I clearly said to myself that this could be the opportunity of a lifetime. But what about Atlanta? What about your six-figures? This place is in the middle of nowhere. You've never been there before. What about your family and how might they feel about all of this? And I began to add up the positives and the negatives. The negatives were outweighing the positives. Nevertheless, my heart didn't care about the positives or the negatives. It only cared about, "Could I make a difference? Wow!

So, I did some tweaking and adjustment to my resume and headed to upstate State New York for a job interview. I also had to explain to my wife that if I got accepted for the job, it would only be temporary at first with limited hours. The per diem position could run anywhere from three months to six months before you got hired on as permanent; if you got hired on as permanent at all. I made it very clear that this was an unsure proposition, with changing variables, included. Well, to make a long story short, they liked me and I liked them and I was hired initially as a per diem (as needed) employee.

Please don't get it twisted, I was truly looking forward to making those six-figures plus per year and more for the rest of my life. I had faithfully served my country in the military for twenty-one years. It was now time for me to take my leadership skills, training skills and human resource skills and nail me one of those nice paying jobs. I knew that working at the entry level position, with these kids was not going to bring me those six figures that I was looking for. So why am I taking a detour and not following the path that has already been laid out for me? That's yet another good question. And yet, the answer was a lot more complicated than just a few word answers and phrases. Nevertheless, I still believe that the man named Mr. Posey had a lot to do with my decision. I will never forget how that one man changed my life forever and how I was in a position to not only change a life, but change a lot of young people's lives. When would I ever get another opportunity like this again in my lifetime? Since, I had no answer, I decided to take a chance. I took a real big chance in hopes that it would pay off. As Mr. Posey took a chance on me and it paid-off, I decided to do the same. Let's do this!

# Chapter 10
# The Right Place, At The Right Time? Yea Right!

**From Military To Civilian To A Big Cut In Pay -- Why Turn Down A Six-Figure Income Opportunity To Work With Troubled Youth?**

When you retire from the military, they say your pay is cut in half. This statement is not true. On the surface, I was pulling in about $68,000 dollars a year income at the time of my retirement from the Army. I would say that two-fifths of that money went to what we in the military call allowances (meals, billeting, Special pays, etc.). When you retire, these allowances are not factored into your retirement pay. Only your base pay is factored in. So, after cutting my base pay in half and taking out allotments for medical, dental, etc., I was receiving just under $20,000 a year in retirement pay. In addition, my wife had also stopped working outside of the home as of 1992. I retired in September 1996. At the time of my retirement, I am the primary income earner for the family. There was no outside money coming in.

Now, let's put things in perspective. When I separated from the Army in June of 1996, I still had three more months of full paychecks coming in until September 1996. This gave me three months to head to Atlanta and get things in place for my family. Notwithstanding, even if I did get hired as a permanent staff at the youth facility within three months, I'd be lucky if I made $30,000 yearly, with overtime. I knew that taking this job at the youth facility was not a great financial move for me coming right out of the military. Going to Atlanta would be a much more lucrative endeavor than staying in New York. Nevertheless, I still chose New York.

    As I reflect on my decision now, I believe I really had no choice in the matter and yet, I had every choice in the matter. As I grew up in Baltimore, I can't help but look back on what and how Baltimore formed who I am and who I am not. Listen, when it comes to Baltimore, I can tell you more bad stories than good ones; there were enough, believe me. Growing up in Baltimore was not pretty at all. As I struggled to overcome, get through the mess, figure out the score, I seemed to always be on the losing side of the equation. Nevertheless, I survived. I found a way to escape the statistical rat-race and not end up like so many before me on those crazy streets. I am truly a success story. So initially, I thought I needed to pack my bags and head to Atlanta to finish the rest of my story. But, that is not what I did and that was not to be my destiny. And yet, there I was in New York and not much better off than when I was in Baltimore. I decided that I was going to stay in New York even though I see and know the difference. I thought, I must be losing my mind.

   Regardless of this impending dilemma, I was already a success story. I grew up in Baltimore, Maryland into a family of eleven kids. Eight of us grew up in one house. We didn't use the word "poor," we used "po." We were so broke that we couldn't afford the "or." Not enough food, not enough money, not enough clothes, not enough of anything. We froze in the winter and we sweated in the summer. Being from such a large family meant that nothing much of anything was left after it came into the house. I seemed to always want more and need more. As the middle child, I never felt like I fit in. To make matters worse, I also saw too many minorities, both young and old, become societal statistics. I was determined that this vicious cycle would not become my fate. I spoke to you earlier about a sixth-grade teacher who changed my life and told me that I was somebody. Determined not to fall through the cracks of the ghetto, I worked hard in school and graduated with honors. When I realized that I was not ready for college after my first year out of high school, I enlisted in the United States Army. I then chose to stick around there for 21 years and then retire.

   I had broken the mold. I had become the exception and not the norm. No statistics for me. Atlanta, here I come for the rest of my story. But that was not to be. It would also not be the end of my story. I knew in my heart that this was the opportunity of a lifetime. I also knew that I might not ever get a chance like this for the rest of my life to help kids just like me. Call me crazy. Call me stupid. But, I felt that I had no choice in this matter. So, based on my heart and my gut, I just had to go for it. As I reflected on my own evolution growing up in Baltimore, I knew that there were no mentors, no guides, no maps, no textbooks to show me how to avoid those inevitable pitfalls. All I had was that sixth-grade teacher and a dream. These kids weren't any different than myself growing up, but the difference they had was me. The only conceivable difference I could see between myself and these kids was that I had never been physically arrested. Everything else was the same. I also knew that no one was going to chastise me for not taking that trip to Atlanta, and taking instead a job that wasn't going to pay me nearly as much money. But regardless, I still accepted the position with the kids. The plight of these kids was calling my very spirit.

Call me soft, call me delusional if you like, but I knew in my heart that if I had gone to Atlanta, I would have questioned that decision for the rest of my life. I had come a long way in twenty-one years and I was determined to give those boys an opportunity that wasn't afforded to me when I was going up. I knew the sacrifice I was making was a huge one, but my failure to not act in favor of those kids would have been an even greater disappointment. It was now or never. So, I said okay, "To the bat-cave, Robin!"

Am I What They Are Really Looking For?

As I stopped and pondered what the job had to offer and what I believed I could bring to the table, there was still the question of would I pass the interview process. Just because I thought I was the right fit, I might not be what they are looking for. In retrospect, I think I know why I didn't choose Atlanta over upstate New York. We all want to make the big money and have a profitable quality of life as we head into our senior years. I lived a good life and I served my country with honor and distinction. So, this is supposed to be my time, right? Yet, I also knew this was a very good cause where someone like myself could truly make a substantial difference. I just couldn't avoid that key factor. So, armed with all of these understandings and positive affirmations, I felt extremely strong and confident as I was about to take the trip for my job interview. I also needed to be up front and candid as we move forward. Everything that happened to me after my interview, was not completely shared with me or even hinted to me during my interview. I'm not saying that I would not have accepted the job with this additional knowledge, but there are some things that I believe I should have been told ahead of time and was not. I speak more about this in Book 2. To be honest, I don't know exactly what they were looking for. Here is what I did know within, I was uniquely qualified for the position. So, in retrospect, I am glad I got selected.

# Chapter 11
# So What Have I Gotten Myself Into

The Pre-Interview

    I was interviewed and briefed. I was also told before I arrived at the facility, what it was going to take in order for me to be successful, or so I thought. Every fiber of my being told me that I understood what I was up against. Yet, regardless of all of that, I knew I could still help change kids. I could still make a difference. Although I was very noble and honorable, I was also extremely naive in this matter. I had no clue what I was really up against, what was really going on and what it was going to take for me to get through it. In other words, I was just plain ignorant. No, I was stupid. In retrospect, sometimes stupidity is a good thing. Because I was totally unaware of what I was really up against, I stepped right into the fire without hesitation. I wasn't looking for the negative and I didn't see any negative. I was told what I needed to hear and it sounded good. By the time I realized I was in the midst of the flames and a mine-field, it was already too ate. Now what was I going to do? So why was I really there and what had I gotten myself into? These are very good questions. Do you have any answers? I'm still looking for some.

The Interview

Wanting to make a difference and truly making a difference are two totally separate things. In my past, I have experienced obstacles, hardships, hopelessness and helplessness. I knew these relatable exchanges could truly help me in the process of identifying with the youth, but it was no guarantee that those experiences alone would give me the ability to actually reach the youth. You see, I grew up surrounded by drugs, but I had never sold or used drugs. I had never been in a gang. In addition, I had never assaulted anyone nor been arrested. The first time I had ever been fingerprinted was when I joined the United States Army. The majority of the kids at the facility, smoked weed; 70-80% sold or were with someone that sold drugs. Most of them lived in single-family homes or within an absentee parent home. Most of them have either dropped out of school or were in the process of dropping out of school. Others were in a lower grade-level in school than they should be. A lot of them either had a gun or access to get one. Most of them lived in the ghetto or the projects. Some were HIV positive, but the staff didn't know. For the most part, it was not their first time having an adverse encounter with the juvenile justice system of New York State. With all that said, I knew I was getting the good, the bad and the ugly. But something inside of me kept telling me that I could make a difference and what I knew about the kid's past, didn't make a difference as it pertained to what I had to do. But then again, had I bitten off more than I could chew? Time will surely tell.

The Post Interview

The interview went very well. Something that stood out in the interview process and caught my attention was that my wife was invited into the interview as it was taking place. Her input was consolidated at the completion of my overall interview. I thought that this part was very interesting. She was invited to come, but I had no clue that she would be invited into the interview process. Interesting. I received a phone call a few days later, letting me know to expect a letter of acceptance with instructions for reporting to work and the date.

When I initially arrived to work at the facility, I thought my main focus would be on the overall dysfunction of the inner-city kids and how I might be of service in helping them. Folks, let me tell you that I learned very quickly that nothing could have been farther from the truth. Based on my initial briefing, I also presumed that the staff were going to set the appropriate examples to and before the kids. I even believed that if I got stuck or needed assistance, coaching or just back-up, my fellow staff members would be there in a heartbeat. I quickly learned that I was delusional. The long story short; the kids weren't the only ones with problems and they weren't the biggest problems either. That's right, I said it. If you decide to read Book 2, I go into depth about the fellow staff, the system itself and the unfortunate failures that surrounded this entire process. I realized that my overall purpose here was bigger than the distractions. My priority was the kids. If I didn't come up with a plan of attack, there was ultimately going to be a train wreck. That's right, a train wreck, which I avoided, but you will have to get the details in Book 2. Sorry.

# Chapter 12
# Expectations

I knew that being successful at the facility and with the kids meant having an understanding of the ground rules. Buying into the basic concepts meant that as a facility we were a team. We were a team with one primary goal - the success of the kids. I had no reason to believe otherwise. I was open and receptive to whatever it was going to take to ensure my success while working at the facility. Below, I've outlined the basics of what was to be done and expected while at the facility. And although some of these concepts were new to me, I believed they were achievable and doable. I was on board. I was all in.

When I interviewed for this position, I was given the basic run down of the facility; the kids that were there and what our mission was as it pertained to the kids. Before they reached our facility, most of these kids had committed a criminal offense and the evidence said they are guilty. They would usually get between 18-24 months of juvenile correction time. Nevertheless, the judges in the cases would give the kid a choice to come to the facility for 6-months and then return home. The other option was to take an unusually larger sentence. For most of these kids, it was a no brainer. They took the 6 months and ran. Notwithstanding, they failed to tell the kids that the facility they are headed to had a man there named, Jerome Redd. And as a direct result of this culmination between the kids and myself, it became a life-changing event. Not just life-changing for them, but also for yours truly. I had no clue as to what was about to take place. There was no way I could have imagined the impact on their lives or even on my own life, when I accepted this job. I just wanted to be able to make a difference.

In addition, I was also given a basic outline or premise as to how the facility would work and its overall objectives. This upstate facility was a six-month in-house placement program, while we also had another 6-month after-care program in New York City. Our overall goal at the facility was to get them changed, prepared, converted, equipped, etc., for the upcoming after-care program. Call it what you want, but after these four stages and six months here, each kid was supposed to be ready to depart and be re-acclimated into mainstream society. I was also told how I and others around me would play a role in this process. It became very clear to me that if I played my role right and moved up within the facility, I would be in a position to have more status and influence in the lives of the kids. This would help increase their ability to acquire the necessary mental and behavioral skills to be released back into society. When the kids arrived, they had six months to go through the four stages at the facility, plus an additional six months, and four stages back in the city. This program used the basics in its implementation or what we like to call the ABC's (Actions/Behavior/Consequences). You've got to pay the cost to be the boss. This made it very simple. So, if a kid messed up at the facility before it was time for him to leave, he just got more time before he left. If a kid messed up once he got back into society, he was either threatened or sent back to the facility for more time. Note, if a kid got sent back or held up, it wasn't considered another or an additional charge to their record. If a kid washed out, he was put back into the "regular" juvenile justice system. That was not good for the kids nor the system.

Due to my military background, there was no need to train me in how to take charge, give commands and/or follow instructions. These attributes came with me to the facility. There was also a physical component to the curriculum, which was directly compatible with my time in the Army. All movements and sessions were organized and held within certain time constraints. At times, I would be expected to take charge and lead a program. While at other times, I was expected to assist with conducting necessary teaching and instructions as laid out within the curriculum. None of this was new to me. This is going to be a piece of cake. Where and when do I start? Not!

Now in addition to accomplishing what to me were the basics, I was also told that there would be more expected of me. While in school during the day, these kids would receive homework and assignments from certified teachers. I was expected, after hours, to assist them, but not do their homework for them. This was something that I also welcomed. In addition, the Director, Assistance Director, First Sergeant, Psychologist and even the Counselors would conduct something called "MAGIC." (MAGIC was conducted to go beneath the surface. They were usually one-hour sessions with open dialogue about feelings, opinions, ideas, concerns, etc.as it pertained to the overall welfare of the kids). If these sessions were successful, there would be times when the kids would call upon us, the staff or inquire of us for input, based on what took place within those sessions. I found out later that the Director and the First Sergeant were very, very effective with their sessions and the kids truly benefited a lot from their specific encounters. If a staff was paying attention, it was easy to tell when you came on shift whether MAGIC had been conducted that day. The kids would ask very personal and even intimate questions of you about your life and theirs. Some kids did it to push your buttons and some did it because they were truly looking for real answers that they didn't have a clue about or weren't sure of. It saddened me at times how some of the staff would just turn off and wouldn't engage the kids who were sincere, looking for honest answers, and genuine responses to their life's problems.

Aside from the academic position, along with MAGIC, we also included some personal and life-skills teachings. This included how to survive in the forest, obstacle courses, basic manners, how to read a newspaper for housing, a job or a major purchase; and, even the place settings on a table. We also did some military training, like Drill and Ceremony and Physical Fitness Testing.

Between the academic classroom, MAGIC, and basic life/survival skills, each of the kids would move from Stage 1 through to Stage 4 and then to the After-care in New York City. Like every new kid that arrived would started out in Stage 1, so did every new staff member. That made perfect sense. As a new staff, I was expected to learn and know all phases of each program. But this would only come with time and practice. I wouldn't be effective in Stage 4 of the operation, if I'd only been working up to Stage 2. I was also told when I arrived as a new staff I was expected to speak very little and just watch and listen. Once the senior staff felt I was getting the hang of things, they would then pass it on to the upper leaders that I was ready for more responsibility. If you asked some of my fellow staff members about me, they would tell you that I got off on the wrong foot. I spent too much time talking and not enough time with my mouth closed. When I was confronted about this short-fall, I just reverted back to our basic mission statement about engaging them verbally, instead of just getting up into their faces, yelling or just dumping them on the floor. It also became very apparent to me that it was easy to dump a kid on the floor, but it took a lot of effort and energy to engage the kids in conversation and then watch the transformation. I called this, having more than one tool, in your tool-box. In my opinion and based on my involvement, much more got accomplished when there was a competent exchange of dialogue between staff and the youth. In the eyes of some of my fellow staff and leaders, I took too much time talking. In their eyes, my talking was a waste of time. What I found interesting was that very few of these folks were willing to convey their concerns to my face directly. Nevertheless, they had no problem conveying these concerns to each other and to the leadership of the facility. Interesting. I speak more on this in Book 2.

**Missing In Action**

The facility was set up in a boot camp style for operational purposes. It had a chain of command and resembled a military model for its programming. The kids were like entry level privates and I would be considered a young Sergeant just coming on board to train and guide them. We all wore military style uniforms at the facility. To be a correction's officer over the kids required prior and/or present military service. This place was set up just like basic training for new civilians coming into the regular military from the outside. Nevertheless, the facility was set up for male juveniles only. Now, some of the staff were females, but not the kids. Let me take a moment to express the following. I am sharing actual accounts of activities and interactions with male kids only at the facility. Yet, the truth and reality were that my experience and observations crossed all sexes and/or gender lines. I also hope that those who read this will glean the true essence behind the fact that I was operating in a facility.

According to protocol, there was supposed to be a minimum of a 1:8 ratio of staff to kids. The facility was staffed by shifts to a 1:10 ratio. Since one staff member seemed to always be doing something or having to go somewhere away from the kids they were supposed to be supervising, it was usually a 1:18 or 1:20 ratio most of the time. Let me be honest, for more than half of our staff at the facility, this 1:18 ratio was dangerous. This goes back to having the lack of appropriate tools. Let me also state that the kids knew what the appropriate protocol ratio of staff to kids was supposed to be. The kids took plenty of advantage of this discrepancy. Most no-touch violations, altercations and the need for physical restraints, occurred when there was just one staff present. Not surprising.

Here is the reality check. Not only was it an all-male facility, the staff at the facility was 97% Caucasian and the kids were 98-99%

minority. So, I thought being a minority myself and being from Baltimore, helped. But that alone, in and of itself, didn't carry a lot of weight when it came to the kids. With them, you had to keep it 100. Being Black and being from Baltimore wasn't enough to give me a pass. Neither was I looking for one. I knew that I had to earn their respect and vise-versa. The fact that I am at least a minority, I think helped me get my foot in the door with the kids. They would at least talk with me and open up to me if for no other reason than to just test the waters. They wanted to see who they were dealing with. They had to put me to the test. In addition, I also believed that their opening up to me was more about self-preservation. They needed to know whether or not they could trust me. If I was a phony, a hypocrite or an Oreo, they would have shut down on me, with the quickness. I understood very clearly that being a minority staff at the facility gave me some advantages, but there were also some restrictions that went with that. Oh, and by the way, some of the real smart kids would use that advantage against me if I wasn't careful. Just because I'm Black or just because I'm a minority didn't give me any special favors with them, period. I still had to prove to them who Jerome Redd really was. Even with this apprehension, my gut kept telling me that I could do this. It wasn't going to be easy, but I could do this. One of the insights I possessed was that if I didn't allow them to see who I truly was on the inside, they would never trust me. Without that trust, I knew that I really couldn't be of service to them or to the purpose that I was hoping to achieve. The term transparency was not a catch-phrase. It was a reality for me. I knew that they were going to pull back every layer to see what I was really made of. So, here goes.

# VOLUME II

## You Know How To Survive. I Want You To Learn How to Live

# FIXING THE BROKEN
## WITHOUT BEING BROKEN
### TURNING ON THE LIGHT, SO THAT CHANGE CAN TAKE PLACE

## JEROME REDD

# Chapter 13
# Forget The Appetizer. Are You Ready For The Entrée?

    I had no idea how my first encounter with the kids was going to be, but I knew I had to be ready. I knew I had to be strong and ready for rejection. They weren't just going to let me walk in. I had to prove that I belonged and deserved a chance to reach them. So, before I could expect the kids to reach out to me, I knew that I had to reach out to them first. I had to tell them who I was and share my background. I had to make it clear to them what my expectations were. In addition, I had to make it perfectly clear to each kid that I would always keep it 100. And, I expect the same in return. If they failed to give me the truth, there was no way I could respond to them, truthfully. This mantra became much more powerful as we got to know one another. I had to establish some basic boundaries. Above all, I needed to make it clear to them that I was trustworthy. I knew that for me these things were not going to be hard to do, but that may not be the case for everybody involved. Just because they could trust me, didn't mean that I was the one they would trust. Real trust comes with time. I needed to be honest and patient with them. They needed some time and six months was perfect. As I began to work with others at the facility, I realized very quickly that to maintain these values was not as easy as it sounded or as I had laid them out. But, wait one minute. That was also not my fault.

**The Set-Up**

Even some of my fellow staff-members were struggling with trustworthiness and transparency. Some of them became easy targets for the kids. But regardless, I stayed focused on the kids. Once the basic foundation was laid, I felt the only thing left was growth. From thereafter, I gave example after example of those interactions which precipitated that growth. There was not any particular order of occurrence, except the beginning. I had to start somewhere. I want the readers to be able to go anywhere within the headings and be able to pull out a section that pertains to hopefully what you are going through, instead of having to read everything to get what you need. I didn't cover everything and I couldn't remember everything. What I attempted to do was give you a variety of examples and incidents that might help as you move forward in your own one-on-one encounters. Be mindful, this is basically the kids and myself doing what we did. There were other things, factors and people who influenced and affected this overall process. I will talk about this more in depth and details, in Book 2. So, don't be discouraged if you get to the end of a session or two and feel like there should be more. There is more. Nevertheless, what I am giving you in Book 1 is more than enough to get you started and to get you going. Pay close attention to one-on-one and group sessions where I found different ways to push and stimulate progress from the kids. Book 2, then takes everything to another level. With that said, we are now ready to explore further the long version. Okay. Let's get this party started.

**Just 2 Things**

I was armed with honesty and openness. These were my entrees. Why? This is what Mr. Posey used on me. I made every encounter a learning experience for both parties involved. I refused to take any experience for granted. I trusted the formula and it worked. In a moment of reflection, I suddenly realized who I was, why I was there, and what the State and those running the facility wanted from me. I also believed I possessed that ability and attributes to be successful and give the powers that be what they desired in the process. Notwithstanding, there was more. There was much more. I knew within that if I only gave them what was required of me and that alone, it would ultimately be a travesty. I had so much more to offer and the kids had so much more that they needed. Sounds to me like the perfect combination or the "perfect storm." So, the question was how do I take these two separate concepts and combine them in such a way to still make progress, while also getting the job done? When I started this journey, I did not have the answer. Yet, when I finished it, I was very successful, but I didn't know at the time how I obtained those answers. I also didn't ask those who were supposed to have the answers for help, either. That was a smart move on my part. Now that was interesting. Yet, the "how to" came much later.

Armed with the basics, I began wondering, where should I start? How do I start and will that be enough? What to do? What to do? Since these were just some of my options, and I had others to choose from, where to start was difficult. So, I decided to start at the beginning. I knew there were some things that were not in question and I decided this would be a very good place to start. You see, here is what I knew. I knew that each of the kids had value. I knew that in their own eyesight, most of them believed they were important. I also knew that each kid had something to offer. They had something to offer to me, to each other, their community and the world. But most of all, they had something to offer to themselves. I also knew that the answers lied within. It had now become my job to find a way to explore, exploit and bring to the surface what many of them didn't even know was there. And in most cases, what was buried just below the surface. Where did this conviction come from? How was I able to ascertain this hidden treasure and why was I so sure that I was absolutely right? See, I had the perfect example years ago with Mr. Posey in the sixth grade and the kids were no different than I. That one example, the one encounter with Mr. Posey, changed my life forever. I knew with the kids that at least I had a starting place. And, if that was good enough for me, why not for them. So, I dove right in. One of the mantras that I would share with each kid boiled down to two of the following. I am only here to do two things and two things only.

-1st thing: <u>I'm here to share information with you.</u>

-2nd thing: <u>And to make you think.</u>

**Things 1 & 2a: My 1st Encounter**

**Here's what I told the kids --**

"That's it, plain and simple. I am not here to tell you how to do it or what to do. I'm not here to give you a game plan for life. These two things I have to convey to you are not mandatory. Neither are they a requirement. You can either receive them or dismiss them. It is solely, your choice. They are not concepts, formulas or truths from academia. These are just some of my life experiences that might or might not help you. You can take all of it, some of it, or none of it. This is your life and your future. You have to find what fits for you. Think about this. If I tell you what to do or give you a game plan for when you go back to NYC and that fails, you get to blame me. But, if you come up with your own game plan and it fails, the only person you get to blame is yourself. Now, let that sink in for a moment. I'm the adult and I'm over you. I'm in charge of you. I even get to tell the powers-that-be, whether you are ready to go home or not. But what I don't get to do is to decide what your game plan is for when you get home. So, how do you like me now? Since this is your life and this is your game plan, what is your game plan? Hello!"

The majority of the kids who left the facility and headed back to the city, didn't have a real game plan. What most of them had was a lot of lip-service and ideas, and that was about it. See, Mr. Posey didn't ask me for a game plan back in the day. He just showed me that I needed one by the life he lived and the way he carried himself. And let me tell you, I needed one bad. Now here comes the Sermon. "See, it isn't that you planned to fail. You failed to plan. You need a game plan. It is a necessity." I challenged the kids that once they returned back to the city to contact those previous detainees and ask them about their success after being locked up at the facility. I bet you each one of them who was successful had a concrete game plan. I explained that a person with a game plan has an automatic advantage over the person who does not. And here is why. If you've got game plans A, B, and C, let's say, plan A isn't working or doesn't work. At least you've got a couple of other options. You can either tweak plan A or get rid of it and do something different. You now have the option to still work with plan A or switch to plan B or maybe plan C. One of the things in life that you can always count on is change. Whether you want it to or not, life will step up and bite you right in the butt. Oh, and by the way, life will change when you least expect it to. If you've got a game plan, then you've got something to fall back on once things get back to normal. But if you have no game plan, you are already in real big trouble. So, when things change or fall apart, all you have then is a bunch of chaos and confusion. Please do me one big favor. Get a game plan. But please, get one that works. Get one that works for you. Below is a story that brings home the idea of why it is so important to have a working game plan and not just any game plan. Speaking of a game plan, if you don't have a game plan, life or somebody will give you one.

### Things 1 & 2b: The Stranger That Knew the Real Me

This is my personal sad, yet true story. I felt compelled and motivated to share this little story with the kids. It happened when I was nineteen years-old and stationed at Fort Hood Texas. It was then that I realized I personally didn't have a game plan and I was letting other people in my life decide who and what I should be. You see, I was raised in the church. I wasn't saved at the time, but I was visiting the military chapel on base. A Major, I had never met before, asked me if he could help me. I said no thank you. I went on to explain to him that I was just visiting to see the difference between my church at home and the military chapel. He then asked me to tell him a little about myself. As I began to reply, he said something that caught me totally off guard. He said, I know what your problem is. You don't like yourself. Talk about an eye-opener. "Excuse me," I replied. I do like myself. He said, no you don't and let me explain. He proceeded to repeat to me, word for word, everything I had just spoken to him. He was right. How could this have happened to me? I'm nobody's dummy. And yet, I cried as I listened to a stranger tell me my life story and he had never met me until that very day. When he told me that I didn't like myself, I immediately denied the accusation. But as I listened to the rest of the story, I quickly saw that he was right on the money and I started balling like a baby. How is it that this man who just met me, knows me this well, yet I, who have been living with myself for nineteen-years, didn't know me at all? What a powerful revelation. I then got angry. I got very angry. I vowed that day that this would never ever happen to me again and it didn't. I knew that day I had a lot of work to do on Jerome and it needed to start now. Talk about no game plan. My game plan was in the ditch. So, at the New York facility, I not only challenged each kid to come up with a game plan, I challenged them to make sure that it was truly their game plan and not someone else's game plan created for their life. So, as you can see, right out of the gate, I compelled them to question and to check themselves. Are you who you say you are? Or are you lying to the world and to yourself? No, you didn't? Yes, I did.

## Things 1 & 2c: If You Don't Know, You Better Ask Somebody?

Trust is a huge factor. I knew the kids weren't going to just open up to me unless they trusted me. I also knew that wasn't going to just happen. I needed to create an atmosphere. I knew sharing my story wasn't going to be hard for me, but they had to believe that it was my story. They were smart. They had their own way of testing your story for street credibility. If it didn't match up, you became the target and let me tell you, it wasn't pretty. They got to hear my poverty story. I told them about the eleven kids, drug-filled streets, daily shootings, and so forth. Once I established a reputation of being legit, I had no problem with the kids opening up and telling me who and what they were about. This approach also worked when I wanted to address or share a specific concept or idea with them.

To make this work for me was very simple. I was always letting them tell me stories about themselves, their lives and what was important to them. Due to the trust factor that had formed, it wasn't hard for them to tell me exactly what time it was and wasn't as it pertained to their lives. They were very candid. As I approached each dialogue, I attacked it with swiftness, with dissection and precision, which exposed the good, the bad and what was beneath the surface. I honestly had them at a disadvantage. But, I used it for the good and not for evil. I also knew that if I was going to be successful with reaching them below the surface, we all needed to be for the most part, on the same sheet of music. I knew that I needed to strip away the extraneous ideas or information that was a hindrance to them. I took pleasure in this approach. To reinforce this very simple approach to the kids, I came at them in the form of a question or questions. There was a constant barrage from me of statements like: Really? You did what? Let me see if I hear you right. I must have misunderstood you. You did what to him? So, you did such and such; and then you did such and such? How is that working out for you? Now, here is what was so sweet about this approach. It compelled them to rethink their own actions and thought process, without me putting them on the defensive. Instead of resisting and defending, they put it all on the table and left room open for dialogue. I was simply amazed. As you read further through my different encounters with the kids, this methodology worked every time. It didn't miss. And there is a saying, if it ain't broke, don't fix it. Eat the meat and throw out the bones. I didn't need to attack the whole story, just the part that wasn't serving them.

With this basic concept and approach, it might have appeared primitive to some, but it proved exceedingly successful for the kids, the facility and for me. What about other alternatives or other conceptual approaches? What about them? They may work and they might not work. But, my bottom-line was, the basics worked. The basics worked every time. I had no desire, want or unction to pursue any other vehicle than sharing info and making them think. Why, because it worked? Mr. Posey used this basic concept on me, forty-years ago and it worked. I turned it around and used it in a different environment, but the need was just the same. And although I wasn't sure whether or not it would work, what did I have to lose? Nothing. This is the same reason why I didn't even think about other alternatives to reach the kids. It worked on me forty years ago, it worked at the facility and it works now.

**Things 1 & 2d: 1,2,3,4; You're Not Going To Make It**

Since some of the kids didn't fully understand the significance of having an earthquake-proof game plan, I felt it was my responsibility to put their game plan to the test. I observed that many of the kids were just stuck in a sea of mediocrity. They knew how to survive, but they didn't know how to live. They also seemed to wear a mask for every occasion. The following exercise seemed to always have me guessing whether or not I was getting the real thing from them as I tried to engage them. There were good days and there were bad days. Some brought their "A" game and some didn't. Don't get me wrong, of the guys who did bring their "A" game, some of them were very good. This forced me to fall back on something I learned from my parents in their method of disciplining us. My parents ensured they had our complete attention before they brought down the hammer. This way they didn't have to do it as often. I believe one of my successes with the boys was from directly following in my parents' footsteps when it came to sharing information. One of the exercises I used to ensure that I had their attention was the following. In a class of 18-20 kids, I would start off at the first row in the classroom, pointing at each kid as I numbered them and counted off, 1,2,3,4 down each of the rows, and when I got to the 4th one I would look him in the eye and say, "You're not going to make it." But I would call out his specific name. I then kept doing that until I completed about 2/3 of the class rows and then someone would stop me. You could visibly see how troubling and even traumatizing these allegations were on their psyche. It troubled them at their very core. But you see, I first needed their attention. And now I had it. I had the attention of every young person in the room. I would then say, hey listen? I didn't make this up. These are proven statistics. One out of four of you is not going to make it. So, let's just keep it real. Since one out of four of you is going to be a career criminal anyway, I'm just pointing it out to you now, instead of waiting for later. That's all. I'm just getting it out of the way now. I would then start counting off the kids again. The class would then erupt in disarray with comments like, "It's not going to be me. I ain't getting locked up again. You got the wrong guy." At this juncture and to ensure that I meant business, I would then bring up about 3 or 4 incidents in the past week that could have very easily kept some of the kids from going home or being sent back to the facility, if they were in the after-care program. These tactics were cold, they were hard, they were impactful, but they were, necessary. It was a true reality check. I had everyone's undivided attention. I was then in a position to pass on some valuable information. Whether they received it or pushed it aside, they were then in a position to at least accept it. Mission accomplished. This was an exercise that I did with all four quads at the facility. Some of them got this exercise more than once from me. One hundred percent of the kids wanted to go home, but the reality was that everybody wasn't going to stay home once they got there. One-fourth of them were going to see me or someone like me, again. I had to let them know statistically that the odds were already stacked against some of them, even before they left. That's deep.

 Getting their attention was one thing, but that was only the beginning. This was just one of my ways of shaking the kids up and bringing them back to reality. Once I had shaken the tree, I could see what we were working with. All fruit cannot be handled in the same fashion; although it may come from the same tree. Knowing the status and condition of each piece of fruit is a huge plus, if you are paying attention. With all eyes focused on me, we could then have a decent constructive conversation about life. See, I knew that most of them wanted success, but didn't have a clue on how and what to do to find it. I also knew that I was not going to make a difference within them, if I didn't know how to reach them at the very core of who they were. In order for me to reach them at their core, I knew I had to pull out the big guns. These are what I call the big three. And the big three, don't play. I had to pull out my sniper rifle and zero in my scope when it came to the big three.

*NOTE: When you look at the "Just 2 Things & The Big Three" understand this, they have nothing to do specifically with just being incarcerated. But, they have everything to do with a person's mind-set, whether locked up or free. Please keep this in mind while you are continuing on this journey.*

# Chapter 14
# The Big Three

Every kid who crossed my path in the facility was given the big three over and over and over again. Was I redundant? You better believe it. Was I relentless? Absolutely! I made it very clear to each child. If you can't answer the big three by the time you leave here, you are in a whole lot of trouble. It was as f I was a broken record; but I needed to be. I personally believed that knowing how to answer these three questions was going to be the key to their freedom and ultimately, save their lives. I truly believed that every kid who expected to be successful at the facility, needed to be able to answer affirmatively these three questions.

1. Why are you here?

2. What is it going to take to get you out of here?

3. What is it going to take to keep you from coming back here?

I also made it clear to each of the kids that I believed these three issues or objectives needed to be known and understood by each and every young man if they expected to be successful. That pertained to their specific incarceration and ultimately beating the juvenile justice system for good. If you take away the incarceration aspect, these three objectives also mimic everyday life. I have to know where I am and how I got there. I have got to know how to move forward from there. And lastly, I have got to also know what it is going to take to keep me moving forward and not regressing. I so wanted them to see that it wasn't their condition that was the problem, it was their perspective. Everything starts in the mind. A good example of what I was trying to say is as follows. It's not what people call you that matters. It's what you answer to. You can't let people take your power. You have to give it away. Too many of us give it away for free and then wonder why we fail so easily. We let too many people take our power and abuse it, when we knew they didn't deserve it to begin with. And why did we do that? Because in many cases we wanted their approval and acceptance.

These three points are not hard to understand or grasp. Nevertheless, I learned as I engaged the young men that too many of them didn't have the correct solutions to these three questions. I quickly realized that I had my work cut out for me. Too many of the kids found themselves toggling between excuses and reality. I wanted them to firmly know that ignoring reality doesn't change the outcome. Just acknowledging it alone doesn't make it better for them. And, blaming others was nothing more than a cop-out. I made it clear to each of the students that they needed to find the answers to all three of the questions, no exceptions. I also made it very clear that only when they knew and understood the answers to all three of the questions were they in a position to come up with a workable game plan to succeed and overcome getting locked up again. I also made it clear to each of the kids that their failure to accurately and adequately understand the three questions, would only leave them at a disadvantage on so many levels of this program, and also in life. The bottom line was, "if you can't answer these three questions when it is time for you to leave here, Then you are an accident, waiting to happen." Translation, there is a very good chance that I will see you again. Wow! Folks, this is not a game. This is real life. This is your life. Hel o!

On the surface, the Big 3, appear to be very simplistic in nature. Nevertheless, the success of any one is directly tied to and interconnected to the success of all three. When I would press most of these kids for the answers to the Big 3, I found many of their answers plausible, but not doable. When it really came down to executing their game plan; putting the rubber to the road, most of them were all talk. This meant that we needed to pull back the curtain and take a closer look. Some of them did not like what we found. And some of them weren't prepared to deal with what we discovered. Too bad, your success in life depends on us dealing with it. And guess what? We dealt with it. Boy, did we deal with it.

The Big 1: <u>Why are you here? What gct you here? Who got you here?</u>

**You Got The Wrong Guy**

When I would challenge the kids with the first question, I always seemed to get either a denial or excuses about how they got to the facility. It was always someone else's fault that they got locked up or it was the fault of their social-economical condition, "I was raised in the ghetto"; "I'm Black"; "The cops got it in for me". So, I would go back to the beginning of the story and ask the very pertinent questions, such as, "Did you sell some weed?" "Were you smoking weed?" "Did you have a gun on you?" "Did you shoplift?" "Did you have a bunch of crack veil on you?" "Were stolen goods found in your possession?" "Was the car that you were riding in, belong to someone other than the driver?" When they would say yes, I would say. "Hey, guess what? You committed a crime, period. You broke the law. So, let's try that once again. Why are you here? "I broke the law." Good. Now we can get started. Is it deeper than that? Of course, it is. But what about the truth? If you don't start with the truth, going behind the scenes to look at other aspects are really a waste of time, because the foundation is based on a lie. Too many of these guys were given a free pass before. So, they didn't have to face the real truth of the matter. In a lot of cases no one held them accountable for the truth or their actions on how they got locked up and ended up there. I had no choice in the matter. I had to confront them. I had to put them under pressure, and I did.

Too many of the guys figured that due to their sad circumstances they should get a free ride or a break when it came to their criminal behavior. I would remind them of my bad situations growing up in Baltimore. I told them that until I joined the Army and met that White Major, at Fort Hood, Texas I was no different. I was just like a lot of them. I used my poor life and my up-bringing as an excuse not to accept responsibility and blame others for my troubles. I explained that others let me get away with this mentality. I made it clear to them that some of them deserved to be locked up; because they were just bad criminals. (Always got a good laugh here.). I went on to say to them that I did some of the same things they did and broke some of the same laws that they broke, but that didn't excuse my behavior. I still broke the law. It's just that I didn't get caught or I was a good talker/liar. I would tell them one of the things I noticed that was different from when I grew up was that I didn't do anything in a group. I did my dirt all by myself. The only witness I had when I got caught was me. And, I like me. I like me a lot. So, guess what? I never testified against myself. I was the only witness.

How is it that so many of these minorities end up in the juvenile justice system to begin with? Good question. Because too many inmates don't have the answer to this one question, the criminal justice system becomes nothing more than a revolving door for the rest of their lives. I feel like I've met the people in the system, outside the system and some of them even in my own family. It appears that their mentality is society owes them something and they're going to take it regardless. The consequences that go with this type of justification is usually against the law. For a lot of the kids that outcome was irrelevant. The end justified the means. So, whether standing before a judge who found them guilty or sitting in their cell after sentencing, many of the kids didn't think what they did was a big deal. I had to do me. And on that note, now you have to do time.

    I made it real clear to each of the kids that they should search their mind and soul and find out why and what it was that put them into the position to get locked up in the first place. Imagine trying to reach out to a kid who believed that the system failed him, society failed him, and his parents failed him. These were the toughest kids to reach, because it was everybody else's fault that they were locked up. I told them that the blame game was not the answer or the solution. And, that if they failed to figure it out, either I would see them again at the facility or the system would. In either case, that was not a good thing for them. I told them to remember their ABC's (Actions-Behavior-Consequences). There is no escape. You have got to pay the cost, to be the boss.

    The Big 2: <u>What is it going to take to get you out of here?</u>

The Big 1 lays out the foundation. Question 2, is what you build on from Question 1. So, now with Question 2, the plot thickens. As a staff, moving the kids through this six-month program, I was at a crossroad. In any given class or group setting, I was basically dealing with two types of kids; those who operated in reality and those who were delusional. It would have been so nice to have the convenience of separating the kids into two different groups and dealing with them separately. But that was not the case. In fact, this dilemma made instructing extremely difficult at times.

Something else I noticed when it came to Question 2. Those who were ready to confront and take on Question 2, would tell me that they didn't know they were going to have to achieve or deal with Question 2. Nevertheless, those who were lost in the sauce, might say something like, "All you got to do is program." Now that might sound really good on the surface, but that was definitely the wrong answer. What was even sadder was when some of the kids' six months expired, they were singing the same old song as when they walked in the door. But guess who got to see them again? That's right, me. There is a saying that I would pass on to the kids that fit this perfectly. "You can pay me now or you can pay me later; but you are going pay me." Anybody can do the program, but doing just the program was not enough. They had to reach within and find their core and expose it. That took hard work and courage. And, nobody can do that for them.

I came to recognize that those who failed to accept responsibility for their own incarceration, usually spent most of their time finding more excuses to add to the ones they already had. Notwithstanding, those kids who stepped up to the plate and said it was me who got me here and I don't have a clue on how to fix it, were the kids for whom I opened their tool boxes and started giving them weapons, nuggets, affirmations and reinforcements that soared them into the stratosphere. Note: There were times when I fell short. There will be times when you get distracted. Don't let it paralyze you to the point of being ineffective. Remember to regain your focus and move on. You've got important work to do. Wipe your tears as you are moving forward.

So, what about the kids who tried to be honest with themselves about their shortcomings? I made it clear to them that knowing why and how they got here was great, but the more important question to ask, was how in the world do I get out of this place? I'm so glad you asked. If they didn't know who they were or what they were made of, they would probably have a problem getting out of there, and once out to stay out. I believe that once they accepted responsibility for their actions, that put them in a position to begin to formulate why they did what they did and could come up with a solution for that. What they needed to do was put in place a substitute for that negative behavior and how they were going to maintain it for the long run. In addition, they had to know who they were and their limitations. Since the place was set up to push their buttons, the kids who didn't know who they were or their limitations, had a real rough time here. You don't have to have all the answers, but you do need to know who you are and have a good game plan. And it's got to be your game plan and not someone else's. As the kids discovered more things about themselves and what motivated them, they took that information and placed it into their game plan's tool box so that it enhanced and built them up. This also positioned them to not tear down what had already been established. It left room for additional attributes and goals.

The Big 2b: Example: <u>He Who Angers You; Controls You.</u>

Speaking of how to get out of here, one of the things that I constantly preached to the young men was that he who angers you, controls you. Why are you giving your power to people who don't deserve it and won't respect it? You must think very little of yourself to allow that to happen. There are those around you who take pleasure in upsetting you and then watching you spiral out of control. Then after you crash and burn, they are the same person who puts their foot on your neck and asks you why can't you get up. For some of those people, their greatest joy is watching you fall apart without them helping you and then blaming you for your ultimate demise. You can't just let other people push your buttons. You have got to know who you really are. If you are not really sure of who you are, then put the mirror of life in front of you and ask yourself this question, "Do you like what you see? Yes or no?" If the answer is yes, keep it moving. If the answer is no, then change it. Below is an example of what can happen when you let other people or things push your buttons.

One day as I arrived on the 3-11 shift, while entering the bay, I heard one of the new staff barking at this young man and I could tell from the young man's response that he was not pleased with this staff. I walked up to the young man and the staff and said, "I know that you are not disrespecting a staff in front of me?" As the young man attempted to explain and justify his conduct, I told him to be quiet. I then instructed him to go into the laundry room because he and I had words that were not going to be pleasant. Note: This laundry room has a nice large glass for you to see in and see out of, but it is basically sound proof. As a result of this tactic, I was able to teach both the young man and the staff a valuable lesson.

As I entered the laundry and closed the door, the young man began to tell me how that staff had disrespected him and he wasn't having it. I very sternly said to him, close your mouth. I posed a question for him to answer. Are you gay?" He gave me a puzzled look. Do you like having men on top of you? (The look on his face was priceless.) Because you were about to be counting tiles on the floor. "Do you know that staff was about to dump you on the floor? How many times do I have to tell you that he who angers you, controls you? As I said these words in a calm voice, I could see the tears running down his face. I then became firm again. I don't want to see your tears. I want to see you think before you act. That is why you are locked up now. And he cried some more. It was a very powerful moment for that young man. He instantly realized that I had just saved his butt from being dumped on the floor and possibly getting 30 more days put on to his time. He also realized that he had allowed someone else to take control of his emotions and actions and the outcome was not going to be pretty. I told him that I am not going to be with him when he gets back to NYC. What are you going to do then? I then told him to remember this. "You have to pay to get into my show. You can't get in for free. Why are you allowing someone who isn't worth it, to drain or take your valuable energy?' I told him that when I send out my energy, it needs to come back to me. Everyone is not going to send it back to you. That can then become wasted energy. You can only send out your energy for so long, when it isn't being returned by others. Those who are worthy of your energy won't steal it, but will return it. You have to be wise enough to know who will and who won't, and then act accordingly. As he apologized to me and for what he had done, I felt good that a positive outcome had taken place. I then cracked the door as if to leave and yelled the following at the top of my voice so that all the kids and that staff could hear what I had to say. "Don't apologize to me. You need to apologize to that staff that I saw you disrespect. Oh, and by the way, that staff better not tell me later that he had any more problems with you tonight. Because if he does, you are not going to be pleased with what I am going to do next. Now get back into program."

Amazingly and without provocation, that young man came out of the laundry room, with a purpose. He approached the staff, at the position of attention and sincerely apologized for his actions. I watched as the staff stood there totally dumb-founded and looking at me as if to say, "What in the world did you say to this kid." I just smiled and went on to the unit that I was assigned to, as if nothing had ever happened. That captured moment was priceless. I was very fortunate at that moment to create an atmosphere that afforded everyone and opportunity for growth. It was moments such as this that compelled me to not quit and keep on fighting the good fight. Wow!

I believe the other thing that took place at that moment was "active listening." (Note: I talk more about this in Book 2). This is not a concept that I hear very often today. I don't consider myself all that special or important. Nevertheless, I've learned the importance of both watching and listening. When this is done well, it is called "active listening." When this concept is properly implemented, you can see things and issues from all sides, not just your side. You can formulate a reasonable plan of attack that can be a win-win for all parties involved. So, when things are going down, don't get caught up. Get yourself in a position where you can be called out or you can step out so that you can see more clearly what's happening. It then becomes a question of not if, but when. You can know how and if it is going to affect you. See, now you are in a position to make choices. You can choose the positive or negative or nothing. But the key is you're not trapped and you're not stuck. Think, before you speak and think before you act. The choice is always yours.

The Big 3a Example: <u>What is it Going to Take to Keep You from Coming Back Here?</u>

Everybody wanted to go home. But the question was, are you really ready to go home? Unfortunately, some of the young people didn't find the answer to that question until after they left the facility. The answer they discovered was that they really needed to stay just a little while longer. So, when it was time to go home, each kid needed to do, what I call, a mental and internal inventory. This would hopefully give them something to work on then and after they left. Even if the inventory didn't look good, most of them were going to be released anyway. That was sad, but a reality. Taking a look inside meant dealing with their baggage. Some baggage is good and some baggage is not so good. But they had to remember that their baggage was their baggage, period. And not confronting that fact wouldn't change it or make it go away. This step took honesty. This step took digging real deep. Everybody wasn't ready or willing to dig deep. But if they were willing to go there, I would go there with them. But I didn't candy coat it. I brought it raw. Because the streets bring it raw. Being successful takes work. Not returning to the facility, also takes work. Now the question becomes, who's going to put in the work? Who's going to step up to the plate and get a hit? Or who's going to step up and strike out? You have got to pay your dues. There are no short-cuts to success. Those who didn't take that inventory seriously, were only fooling themselves. Once the kids returned home, it didn't take long for them to figure out the reality of missing this part of the exercise. And by then, it was too late.

    The young men who returned to the facility, came back for a number of different reasons. Some came back because they weren't ready to go to begin with. Some returned because the support system that surrounded them, was failing them. These failures came in the form of a drug-addicted parent, who was not taking care of their brothers or sisters. This also came in the form of selling drugs to keep from becoming homeless. In those cases we tried to rescue them and get them back to the facility before it got real ugly. Once we had repaired that support system, we returned them to the city for another try. Some failed due to gang-related involvement and/or peer pressure. I also discovered that when most of the young people returned, I was one of the staff they didn't want to talk to. And, I was not mad about that either. They knew I was going to have a specific conversation about their return to the facility. They also knew that the conversation was probably going to be very uncomfortable. I basically became their conscience. As long as they kept it 100, I wouldn't give them any problems. On the other hand, if they tried to play me, then it was time to have some fun. Needless to say, it got ugly. It got real ugly. Below is just such an opportunity.

The Big 3b Example: It Wasn't Me (Just Call Me Shaggy)

Since most of the young people there didn't get to meet one of the kids who returned, having someone like this young man to share their story, could prove to be very valuable to all who were present. So, after I hit the class with the Big 3, I went on to say that we had in our presence a young man who returned to our facility. I asked him to share with the group as to why he had returned. At the time of his confession, I didn't know why he had returned. I never got a chance to approach him until then. He went on to share the following story.

He initially attempted to convince us all that his return was really not his fault. So, I let him tell his story to try to explain his situation. He said he was sitting on his stoop, minding his own business, when a car pulled up in front of his house and he didn't recognize the driver. When he left his steps to approach the car, he noticed that the two guys in the back seat were old friends of his. He then, based on the urging of the driver, took up the invitation and went for a ride in this car. This same car was later pulled over and everyone in it was arrested for riding in a stolen car.

At this point, I stopped his storytelling and said, now let me see if I got this straight. You were sitting on your own steps, minding your own business? Then out of nowhere, this guy, who you didn't know, pulled up in a car that you hadn't seen before? When you approached the car, you did notice that the two in the back seat were old friends of yours, but you didn't know the driver? Then the driver, not your friends asked you to go along for a ride? Now at this moment, it never occurred to you that this car might be stolen? His response was no. (Now here comes that "active listening"). I then asked him what were you arrested for the first time you got locked up? He said driving in a stolen car. I then asked him was he arrested alone? He said no. I said, who was with you? He said that he got arrested with the two guys that were sitting in the back seat of this very car. So, I said, let me see if I got the story straight. You didn't know who the driver was, but you did know the two guys that were in the back seat that you had been previously arrested with, in a stolen car. Now when the driver asked you to go for a ride in this car, it never entered your mind that this car might have been stolen? This kid replied again with a no, it never crossed my mind. At that moment in front of the entire class, I spit on my hand, rubbed it on my forehead and asked the class, "Is the stupid sign gone?" The entire class erupted in laughter and was on the floor. This kid was now none too happy with me at all. But that was okay. Since he wasn't keeping it real with the class and me, I felt compelled to pull his hold card and embarrass him in front of everybody. That thing was hilarious. How could he have believed that I was going to let this mess slide? He must have been smoking some of that good stuff. Other staff might buy that story, but it was full of crap. And, if I hadn't confronted him, he was going to continue to try and sell that same story until it was time for him to go back to NYC and get locked up again. Initially, he was mad with me. But he got over it. He later admitted that he was fronting because he felt like that was the only thing he could do. I was so glad to see him take ownership for his actions and his conduct. I hoped he would put a plan in place so this never ever happened to him again.

Note: It was not my job or hope to make a fool out of this young man. But it was my job and hope to make him honestly confront the real issues. He knew that he wasn't keeping it real and so did everyone else. I also didn't relish pouring salt into the wounds. But it was necessary. Nevertheless, I didn't call him out. I let his own words call him out for all to see. And man, it was pretty ugly. Guess what? I would rather him be mad with me and fix his life, than for him to continue to keep selling that same story to everyone until he got home and got locked up again. It sure felt good knowing I was making a true difference in someone else's life. I not only had to go under the surface on this one. I had to go deep. I had to go real, deep. But he was worth it.

There was a price to pay to get out of there. But there was also a price to pay to stay out of there. If you weren't willing to pay that price, then the system would probably see them again and again. For many of the kids, they were only focused on getting out but not staying out. So, they were not putting anything in place, for the long haul. For me, that was not good enough. I forced them to think and then rethink. Only they knew the answer if what they put in place was good enough.

Understanding and knowing the Big 3 is essential. Nevertheless, I also think there is a piece that you need to add to the Big 3. Are you hungry? Are you willing to do whatever it takes to get the job done or are you just in La La land? Are you that homeless person waiting for a handout? Or are you the person who's not worried about the menu or the price? You already know that you have what it takes to pay the bill, once you've consumed the meal. Oh, by the way, you not only have to be hungry, you've got to stay hungry. There is no place or room for complacency. You have got to keep it moving. There are no free rides.

# Chapter 15
# So What About My Opinion

Too many adults and people in authority have already told them time and time again, who they were and what they needed to do to be successful. I asked, "How has that worked for you?" What those outside of you think of you, have assessed of you and for you, in my humble thought process, is basically their opinion. Now, I have a saying about opinions, goes a little something like this. "Opinions are like butt-holes, everybody's got one and, in most cases, they all stink." So why not have your own? It will smell just as bad. I also have another saying, "If you don't know who you are, someone will surely tell you who you are. "So, tell me, Who are you?" That Major Chaplain, at Fort Hood, Texas, told me who I was. That was so sad. He didn't even know me, but he knew me. He knew my type. You cannot let others or what others think of you, define who you are. You have to know who you are, period.

Some might think that my mantra of sharing information and making you think is too simplistic. I believe that if I give you the answers without options, you are definitely doomed to fail. Yet, if I give my answers to your problems, where is there room for you to insert your own ideas for growth? Even if my input is off the charts and everyone else agrees that it is the creme-de la-creme, how long can it sustain you? Be open, be attentive, but be determined. Be determined to find your niche. Be determined to find what really works for you and you alone. I've got some good ideas. I've got some great ideas. But they probably work best for me, because I've already put them to the test. Don't follow or receive what I have to offer, until you have tested it. If you like it and it works, then make it your own. But please, test it first. And do me another big favor? Watch out for the "blame games."

**The Blame Game:**

When I share information, you don't have to accept it or receive it. My offering is based on what I know about you and what I think might inspire you. I'm also sharing with you what has been shared with me over a lifetime. It isn't necessarily what you really need. But these are real life stories and experiences that I have been through that I think might be of assistance to you. Should I say something that can assist you, feel free to adopt it, try it out and even use it. But if you ain't feeling it, leave it right where you found it and keep it moving. But be sure you come up with something that will work and keep you from repeating your past failures. That way, people won't start thinking or calling you crazy.

Things 1 & 2e Example of Sharing #1:

I realized later in life, that as a youth, I blamed a lot of my bad decision-making surrounding growing up, on me being poor. In addition, I also realized that blaming it on poverty afforded me the convenience of not having to accept the fact that at times, I just made some really bad and stupid decisions. And besides, why should I have to accept responsibility, when I can blame someone or something else? It worked for me. Here's my reality. I didn't have to work that hard when I was in school K-12. And since nobody pushed me academically, I didn't push myself. Without studying or doing much homework, I soared as an A/B student. I even graduated from high school with honors. I felt extremely proud of myself when it was time for me to head to college. Unfortunately, I was in for a rude awakening. So, when I didn't do that well in college, I blamed it on the Baltimore school system and my teachers. Some might say, I was just lazy or even dumb. I don't believe that either of those were true. Nobody, except Mr. Posey, held me accountable. And I wasn't mature enough to hold myself accountable. I realized later that I didn't have the tools or the internal disciples to push myself. So then, who is at fault? Here is what I do know, as long as you keep playing the blame-game, you get to stay stuck in the past and live with the regret. What happens, just happens. I can't and no one else can change the past. You just have to find a way to move beyond what isn't working, so you can establish a way to find your future. I chose to enter the Army after my first year of college.

Guess what? When I retired from the Army, I went back to college. I even graduated with honors with a BS degree in Psychology. Who would have thought? When I stopped blaming others, a weight was lifted from my life. It became lighter and it opened me to other people, places and things in my life. I realized that playing the blame game is a form of wasted energy. It seldom gives you anything in return, except a feeling of uneasiness. You have to find a way to move beyond the blame game. You need to take charge of your destiny and not let others and life take charge for you. So, when a kid tells me that he is locked up because he got caught with weed; lives in the projects or because he's Black; that's the blame game. See, it is okay to break the law if you fall into one of those three categories, right? In addition, that's the same kid who is always complaining that it is the staff who is holding him back in program, and it is not his attitude that is causing him to fail. Of course, a few of them come back from the city, but some can't or won't tell you or themselves why. When a kid came at me with what I think was an excuse, I was not nice. You see, I believed that their life's progression depended on how hard I was on them and believe me, I was hard. See, I knew that even with their excuses, they had to reach within for the solution. I had no choice. I was compelled to make them look within. Some of them found a goldmine. Some of them found quicksand. And some of them found nothing. One day I had a kid tell me that I made his head hurt. I told him, thank you. That's the objective of the exercise. If it was hurting, then it was working. If it was working, then he was thinking. And thinking brought about clarity. I'll settle for thinking any day of the week.

**You're Not The Future, You're My Future**

Things 1 & 2f Example of Sharing #2:

I wanted each of the young men to know that I had a very personal and selfish reason for their success. Both the kids and staff, at times, didn't understand my rationale for how I engaged and purposefully pushed the kids. The following is a candid discussion that I had with classes and groups on more than one occasion. "The reason that I am so hard on you and need you to think is that you are not just the future; you are my future. Translation: 20-30 years from now you are going to be running this country whether I want you to or not. If I fail to invest in you, I condemn myself. So, I have a very selfish reason for taking on this role in your life of making you think and pushing you. Having the correct thought process, could save your life and maybe even save mine. In a nutshell, I am being selfish. The way I treat you has everything to do with my own personal and future outcome. Think about it this way. Some twenty years from now when I am walking to the mailbox to get my social-security check, I want you to be the boy who's helping me across the street, so I can go and cash it.

And not the boy who's busting me upside my head and taking my check from me." The laughter and chuckles after making this statement assured me that most of these kids understood the story and the explanation that came with it. I didn't ask anyone to incriminate themselves, if the shoe happened to fit. Below are a few more candid conversations as well.

1. You've got something that I need. If you fail to give it up, we both lose. Translation: If I tell you that a duck can pull a truck, you need to hook it up. (Note: "But Sergeant Redd, A duck can't pull a truck." But if I tell you it can; watch it move.") Two kids in the program later told me that they saw the duck pull the truck. Hello! I was personally doing back flips. Both of those kids explained what they meant by this and I could tell that they both got it. I didn't know it at the time, but I later realized that the kids were actually validating my worth. Mr. Posey told me and showed me, but the kids validated it. They're actions both at the facility and in the after-care, proved that what I had to offer made a greater difference or impact than anyone ever expected; including me.

2. Forcing these kids to really think for themselves, meant no excuses. Tell it to someone who wants to hear it. Tell it to the Judge. But don't tell it to me. Has life been hard on you?

Is your daddy missing? Is your momma a crack-head? Do you live in the projects? Who cares? You better figure out what you want in life and you better figure it out quick or you'll be stuck, like Chuck? And just like a cooked turkey; you'll be done. All somebody has to do is stick a fork in you. I shared with the kids my own personal background and how I had to step over the junkies to get to school in the mornings. I told them how gunfire was no big deal and when it stopped, you got up off the ground and finished playing ball and carried on like nothing had happened. I talked about my rat-infested, roach-infested, bed bug-infested, lead-based paint-infested homes that I lived in growing up that were falling apart. I talked about me using a wood stove in the city, instead of central heat in the winter and opening window for air conditioning in the summer. I lived under these type conditions, until I left for the Army. I told them how my daddy was there and wasn't there. He was either absent or drunk; pick one. All of these are good excuses for me to turn out bad and become a criminal, but I didn't. Guess what, you don't have to keep the cycle going either? The choice is yours. You can give excuses, but I'm not accepting excuses. How do you like me now?

3. I don't want to hear your excuses or your complaints. Tell me the truth. Keep it real with me or like I've heard it said, keep it 100. If you don't keep it 100 with me, then my response can't be 100. Check this, when you try to take that short-cut, I'm going to peep your hold card and embarrass you in front of everybody. So, if you keep it real with me, then I'll keep it real with you. Promise! If you lie to me, then I will be forced to lie to you. I don't have any choice in the matter. There is no way I can provide you with a true assessment of input, if you give me erroneous information to make that decision upon. For a lot of these kids, denial was the word of the day. If I don't have to accept responsibility for my actions, then I won't. I'm sure not going to let you make me accept responsibility, when I can conveniently blame it on someone or something else. Also, true acceptance means that I have to show my feelings in front of others. Showing your feelings in front of others is a sign of weakness. Those who are weak, become prey and get destroyed. Helping them to see that showing their feelings was not a sign of weakness, wasn't easy at all. In my opinion, it goes back to the trust factor. If they trust you, they will open up to you. If you don't betray that trust, they'll do it more than once. Translation, you're making progress. You

don't have to agree with the kids, but this is the nature of the beast for them. I had more break through with the kids' one-on-one sessions than I ever did confronting them in a group sessions. But I was also successful, in groups. I learned that if you listen and then feed them back their own words in a manner that is clearer than the manner in which they spoke it, it usually hits the mark and they have no other choice but to wake up and confess the error of their ways. This method also allowed a lot of them to rethink their thought process. I call it that "stinkin-thinkin." They think that they have it all figured out, until you throw in that monkey wrench. And it came in the form of a question or two. With only a few strategically placed responses they quickly realize they were off course then and they are still off course now. Once you realize they recognize this flaw in their reasoning, you can now guide them in a direction that can provide options they had never considered. Below are examples of a group sessions where this type feedback took place.

*Note: To those of you who want to use Volume 3 for yourself or the future, I would like to share the following. As I engaged the young men, I made it a point to never challenge their truth, but only examine their harvest. This allowed them to see what type of seeds they had sown. You can't plant oranges and expect bananas.*

# VOLUME III

# Group Sessions/One-on-One's

# FIXING THE BROKEN

**WITHOUT BEING BROKEN**

TURNING ON THE LIGHT, SO THAT CHANGE CAN TAKE PLACE

## JEROME REDD

# Chapter 16
# Let's Talk Money, Drugs and/or Sex

Up until now, I've shared some background information, facility information, kid information, and even personal information. I've talked about the basics, trust, the game plan and accountability. All of this is good and a nice place to start, but there is more. When you choose to take on the mantle of active listening, there will arise pieces, concepts and excerpts that can prove to be of value if you are really paying attention. If you know how to assess, ascertain and formulate this, you can come up with a decent strategy to address these items. And, that is exactly what I did. I noticed as we interacted on a consistent basis the kids didn't mind sharing or opening up to me. This liberty proved to be a wonderful blessing. But, it didn't stop there. Here is what I also noticed. When it came to the subject of money, drugs, sex, women, gangs, respect, these kids lit up like a Christmas tree. These were triggers that caused them to not only speak up, but nearly vomit what was on the inside. It could also escalate and get completely out of control. The realization and acknowledgement of this discovery could either be a curse or a blessing. I choose the latter. I also paid attention to the facility atmosphere, who was running the show doing my shift, and how the staff had run the previous shift. This happened to be important because sometimes you had to spend the entire shift dealing with the outside forces and residue that were already present when you arrived with your agenda. I will talk about this input and influence more in Book 2.

What I have shared with you thus far have been the one-on-one sessions or me addressing a group, and me speaking to each person individually within the group. What I am about to do now is show you how I dealt with the group as a whole collectively. Then I will share how I took a specific teaching point that whoever wanted it or selected it could either use it or leave it be. I truly loved these sessions. I will call these my MAGIC sessions. I spoke about this earlier as it pertained to the leadership of the facility. I hadn't reached those physical titles, but I believe that I was just as effective as the big guns. I believe that these sessions brought out the best in me. And believe me, I had to bring my "A" game. As for the kids, I believe these sessions compelled them to reach deeper within, to reveal their true selves. I believe it also proved that I was truly legit and not just some fly by night-ter off the street. They knew that I had something to offer and in turn, they could benefit from it. Just imagine how that made me feel as a person and as one who had already traveled their journey. Wow!

Group Session 1: How Much Money Does Webster Make?

For a number of these kids, writing a letter home and receiving a letter from home, became the highlight of their day. When the time came to hand out the mail, it appeared that everybody was or wanted to be in compliance. Unfortunately, for about 75% of the kids they were either reading below their grade-level or were illiterate. One of the things the facility provided for them to deal with this issue were dictionaries. Each area had about 3-4 dictionaries. So, when it came time for them to do homework for school or write letters home, these items became very valuable; you would think. I thought that during this time we would have problems with not having enough dictionaries on-hand. But, I was wrong. Sometimes, things got a little ugly, though. See, these youth wouldn't ask for a dictionary, they would ask the staff to spell the word for them. And, in my humble opinion, too many of the staff would just go ahead and spell the word for the young man to get the transaction out of the way. I personally believed that this repeated activity did them a disservice. I chose to take a much different approach to this predicament. It appeared at times to irritate both kids and staff. "Why don't you just spell the word and get it over with?", they would ask.

When I was asked by a young man to spell a word, let's say the word was, "experiment." My reply would be something like this. Are you ready? Once I got the affirmative, I would say w-e-b-s-t-e-r. In most cases, the young man would come back with, "that word doesn't start with a 'w', it starts with an 'e'." I might sarcastically respond, you're kidding, right? Then after they responded, I would repeat the exact same spelling of the word (w-e-b-s-t-e-r.). Some of the kids would get very frustrated with me, by this point. In some cases they had already started writing this in their letter home or in their homework for school and now they have to erase it or draw a line through it. By now, some of them were extremely hot with me. Wanting them to understand the nature of my actions, I then gave the kid one of the dictionaries that had been placed at the podium on their behalf, and I would make the following statement. "Do you know that Webster makes a lot more money than I do? And if I do Webster's job for him, he isn't going to give me any of his money. So why don't I let Webster do what he gets paid to do?" Some of them truly believed that I am just being totally unfair and hard on them, because they were asking for legitimate help and that I was playing games with them. Some would say, I'm just asking you to spell a word. Give me a break? On one hand, I understood their frustration. They had been conditioned. The expectation was that I should be conditioned as well to do what everybody else did. Well, I had an ulterior motive.

I eventually developed a reputation in the quad around homework time that if they wanted to get embarrassed, just ask

Sergeant Redd how to spell a word. I believe that too many of these kids didn't fully understand my rationale or motivation for taking this approach. It was never about embarrassing or exposing them. Knowing that most of them had literacy problems, you would think I would be a lot more compassionate than that. I felt that under the conditions that existed, if I spelled the word, I was doing them a great disservice. I felt instead of helping, I was making it worse. I knew that it was embarrassing, but that was not my objective. Embarrassment was only a by-product of their laziness. If they would have just come to me or asked for a dictionary, I would have given it without fanfare. But, they chose to ignore the tools provided for their benefit and then in turn, chose a poor substitute instead. I was not having it. I also wanted to be an example to correct the staff who spelled the words for them. Since I'm not their boss, the next best thing I could do was to be the example. I hoped my fellow staff members saw, because I never confronted or addressed this directly with staff. As for the kids, even if they had a problem reading, that would be okay. I would help them, but none of them ever said to me that they had a problem reading and asked for my help.

Although, I knew this was sensitive and at times embarrassing, I still stuck to my guns. I knew how important this was and I refused to compromise. What was also interesting about this story is that at times, some of the kids who were confused and knew that I wasn't doing this just to humiliate them, would confront me and ask why I wouldn't just spell the word. My response would be, let me ask you a question? When you finally look up the word in the dictionary, is that the only word you find? They always said no. Did you happen to find new words or other words? Yes. Then I responded, now you know why I always sent you to Webster and not myself. These just happened to be cases where I made them think, and they also got an education at the same time. Webster, can do for you, far more than I could ever do.

    I also shared with them about how they had plenty of time and plenty of books to read, whereas most don't. I told them that when I was their age, I wish someone had given me a love for reading. I was honest and told them that I have read very few books in my lifetime. Yet many of my heroes and sheroes are very avid readers. I told them that books can take you anywhere and places you want to go. They will take you to anywhere in this world and beyond. Mastering the English language is a door-opening tool. Those who become avid readings tend to achieve this feat a lot quicker than those who don't. Read, young man, read. When I reflect back on these episodes, they remind me very vividly of a saying, "Feed a man a fish and he eats for a day. Teach a man to fish and he eats for the rest of his life. Just knowing that, humbles me.

## Group Session 2: Condom Or No Condom? That Is The Question

As I sat in a group circle with the kids one day, the conversation switched to females and respect for females. The conversation started out with the young men saying and telling me, just what they thought I wanted to hear. These types of sessions between us bordered on and were predicated by how much trust was in the atmosphere. But I wanted to know the true mentality of the gentlemen I was dealing with. This required that I dig a little deeper. There were approximately fifteen young men in this circle and myself. With me having the knowledge that a number of them already had babies and were not married, I started the conversation talking about sexually transmitted diseases and HIV. They in turn, gave me the right responses as they understood the need for protection, and whether or not it was on their part to step up or the female's part for protection. I then asked a very important question. "How many of you use a condom, each and every time, before engaging in sexual activity?" Nearly, every hand in the circle, went up. So, then I asked another question. "How many of you have a baby outside of marriage?" At least seven to eight hands went up into the air. Knowing that most or at least some of them weren't being honest with me or the group, I knew I needed to flip the script, and I knew that I had to make it personal. You can't fix what you won't acknowledge.

So, I shared with them a scenario which was similar to an experience that I personally had when I was growing up. I asked them that after I shared this story to tell me what they would do. I then shared the following story. I said, suppose you are interested in this girl, who is fine. She is not a side-piece, neither a chicken-head or any of that. She could even be, "the one." Let's say you walk her home from school every day, but all you get to do is drop her off at the front door. Her mother is waiting there every day for her to come home from school. She and you have only kissed, but you would love to take it to the next level. But the mother is blocking every effort and angle. Momma got you on lock-down. Nevertheless, this young girl is also into you as well. You decided that although you can't do anything right now, she is still fine and you are going to settle for just walking her home every day, anyway. Who knows, one day you might get lucky. And then, that one-day comes. She arrives home from school one day and read the note left by her mother that she has to work a little late, to heat up her food for dinner, and she better not let anybody in the house that doesn't live there. You're thinking to yourself that today, might be your lucky day. You also notice that she is smiling an awful lot while she is reading her mother's note. Because of her mother blocking you on previous occasions, you weren't prepared for this letter. Notwithstanding, you don't have any condoms on you and you can tell that she is ready to do the deed. Then I said to the group of young men, "Show of hands, how many of you would now go to the corner store and buy a condom and how many of you would just hit it and say, I ain't taking no chances, by going to the store?" All of them raised their hands signaling that they would go and get a condom. As a gesture to them of don't play me for stupid, I spit on my hand and then rubbed it on my forehead vigorously and pointed to my forehead and asked, was the stupid sign still there? I then commented to them that I was born at night, just not last night. Although we all laughed at my gesture, there wasn't a thing funny about it. With my knowledge of human nature, adolescent sexual behavior and my own personal experience, I went on to share the following with them.

I felt the liberty to pull back the curtain, put the cards on the table and tell it like it is. More than half of the young men had at least one baby and some had two that they are not taking care of, because society is taking care of them. I also believe that the talk that every young man and young woman should have about sex is probably lacking in at least 50% of those sitting around in this group. So, I not only confronted them, I took it deeper and I made it raw. Let's just say, I got up front and very personal with these young boys. I shared this story so that they would know that I had been where they are and the possible consequences that could occur when your libido is not in check.

## Busted - Where's My Libido?

I told the group, maybe things have changed since I was your age, but if the shoe was on the other foot, I know that I wouldn't take a chance on mom coming home while I was at the store, or her coming to her senses after I left to go to the store or her girlfriend calling her to talk her out of it. I'm getting the booty and I'm getting it right now. I ain't thinking about HIV, I ain't thinking about sexual transmitted diseases and I definitely ain't worried about no baby or pregnancy. The only thing I'm thinking about is that if I don't hit now, I might not ever get a chance to hit it again. And as I'm telling this story about not having self-control and discipline over my own sexual conduct, you could hear a few of them laughing, while the others were smiling. They knew that they were no different than I. They knew that I was keeping it 100. And they knew that I was telling the truth about them. Hello!

I then went on to say that I wasn't sharing this with them to accuse or belittle them, but I wanted them to understand that there are normal consequences which coincide with their regular behavior. But there are also irrefutable consequences when it comes to sexual conduct. I wanted them to know that there is another side to this lack of self-control when it comes to sexual activities. I went on to share with them the story about a young woman in her early twenties who not only set me up, but took full advantage of my lack of sexual control in this very area. I was home on vacation from the Army for a few weeks. Like a few of my other friends, I called her to let her know I was in town and maybe she and I could get together before I left. Note: We were both attracted to each other physically, but we never had sex in the past. It just didn't work out and now I'm in the Army. She told me that this Friday was her birthday and she had promised to babysit for her older sister. She told me that it would be nice if I at least stopped by and wished her a Happy Birthday before it got too late. I thought to myself that this was no big deal, but I was wrong. I fell right into her trap. When I arrived Friday evening, at around 7 pm, her sister and husband were departing for the club. I thought they were going to be leaving around 8pm. I then went into the kitchen and turned on the television to watch a Baltimore Orioles home-game. I hadn't seen one of these games in years. She then went upstairs to make sure that the kids were in bed. Now the plot thickens. When she returned downstairs, she sat in the living room and put on a Smokey Robinson record and yelled at me in the kitchen to come into the living room. I replied that the game was good and that I was enjoying it. When that was not enough to move me, she came to the kitchen door and asked me again to come into the living room. At this point, I could tell she was serious, but I had no clue how serious. She then walked in front of the television and blocked the set and when that didn't work, she turned off the television. She said that I came over to wish her a Happy Birthday and not to watch television. So, she grabbed me by the hand and led me into the living room and we sat kind of facing each other on the couch. Here comes the moment of truth. We went from kissing, to getting buck-naked on the floor, and engaged in sexual intercourse.

Wait just one minute. I only came over here to wish her a Happy Birthday and maybe get a kiss. I purposely came by early, because she gave me the impression that her sister and husband weren't leaving until about 8pm and the kids weren't going to be in bed until 10pm, because it was the weekend. None of that was true. After being coerced into the living room to talk about her birthday, I am now engaged in sexual activity. The issue of protection and consequences hadn't been uttered from anyone's mouth. Oh, but it's coming. At the moment, just before she was about to climax, which would automatically make me climax, she uttered the following words, "I'm not taking any protection." The only intelligent thing to do at ~~that~~ a moment like that would be to pull out. I didn't. See, I wasn't that intelligent. I also believe that most men under the same circumstances wouldn't have pulled out either. But we're not talking about most men. We're talking about me. I don't get a pass. What I did was still not okay. What I did was stupid. I still had a choice. I still had a responsibility. "Now, don't get me wrong, that's what you call low-down and dirty. She set a brother up big time. She practically raped me and then waited until I was ready to seal the deal, to tell me she wasn't taking any protection. At the moment of release, I realized what had just happened to me and I had no one to blame, but me. This was not her fault. She took full advantage of my lack of sexual control and lack of sexual responsibility. Shouldn't I have been thinking about a sexually transmitted disease? Shouldn't I have thought about the possibility of becoming HIV positive? What about a possible pregnancy? I have a saying that fit this scenario. "God looks out for fools and drunks. And in this case, I wasn't drinking." Of course, the young men wanted to know what ultimately happened after that situation with this girl. Knowing that the possibility now existed that she could be pregnant and I could be the father, we had the following conversation, since I would be leaving in a couple of days to return to my base at Fort Hood, Texas. I told them that I told her that if she became pregnant and the child was mine, I would take full responsibility for it and her pregnancy, but there was going to be a paternity test once the baby arrived. I had a very close female friend who lived in Baltimore who told me that she would monitor things while I was in the Army and would be my liaison with this matter, if needed. After I returned to my military base, I held my breath for about a year. She didn't get pregnant and my friend didn't need to exercise her oversight duties. Thank you, God.

Even though I didn't have to bite the bullet, I'm not proud of how this situation happened to me or turned out. The outcome could have been a lot different. I learned later that she was very sexually active and was purposely trying to get pregnant. I wanted the young men to have a real-life example of when you don't take control over your sexual urges, life will. The outcome can be devastating. As I told this story to these young men, I was about 45 years-old with no kids. At the time of this incident, I was about 21 years-old. What if she had gotten pregnant. I can only imagine how different my life would be with a 24 year-old adult child now. I told them that thinking with the wrong head could prove costly.

Group Session 3: Oh Yeah, I Hear You, But She's Not My Sister

When it came to the opposite sex and how some the young men viewed women, they definitely had a distorted view. In addition, a number of the staff were puzzled and bewildered by their view and how they talked about women as a whole. Now, as I reflect back on how some of the staff felt about the young men and how the young people felt about the opposite sex, I can truly conclude the following. I would convey to my fellow staff-members this. How can we expect these young kids to respect other lives or the opposite sex, when they, in many cases, don't respect their own lives? It really didn't surprise me how the young men treated and spoke about women. I was not really upset with the prospective that so many of them took, when it came to the female of the species. These young men relegated most females to the level of a side-piece, chicken-head, wif-fie, Boo and so forth. None of these are terms of endearment. These names reflect that women are less than and not equal in their eyes. If I don't love myself, how can I attempt to love someone else? If I have no self-respect for me, then where am I going to find the respect needed for others, especially women? It became very clear to me that some of the staff were also part of the problem. If they couldn't figure out what the kid's problem was, then they were not capable of providing the kids with the proper resources or tools to deal with their problems. And yes, females were a big problem to the young men. I was amazed at times to see the look on the staff's faces when I shared this revelation about the kids needing to love themselves first. My only hope was they took a different approach as they dealt with them in the future.

But I Was First

I could tell that in the eyes of some of the young men, they felt men are better and deserve more than women. One day while the kids and I were talking about females and the difference between them and young men, something interesting happened. One of the kids in his excitement and desire to show off for the rest of the boys told this story. He said Sergeant Redd, my boys and I had this chicken-head one time and we ran a train on her (Definition: Everybody had sex with her, one after the other or at the same time). He then said, but I went first. (This shows that he's the Alpha male or at least in the top leadership position, compared to the rest of his boys). Appalled by this statement, I knew that if I responded the way I wanted too, he would only become defensive and shut down. So, I knew that I had to find a way to reach inside and show him that he had nothing to be excited about or proud of. I needed to find a way to make him see just how disgusting what he said really was. I also believe I was successful in that pursuit as I went after this young man in a way that he wasn't prepared for nor was I sure of what the outcome would be when I finished.

I said to this young man, "So you got to go first, wow. Okay, so obviously, you don't have any sisters, right?" He responded, "Yes, I have two?" I said, "You must be kidding, two?" He responded, "Yes, two." I said, "then that they both must be younger than you". He said, "no, one is younger and one is older". I then said, "well they both must be ugly". And he said "no, they are both beautiful." Then I said, "they must not have a boyfriend." He said "the oldest sister does have a boyfriend." I said "well, how does the boyfriend treat your sister?", and he replied "very well." I said, "what would you do to the boyfriend, if he did anything to hurt or mess-over or disrespect your sister?" He responded that he would kick his "you-know-what." I said, "really? You would kick his behind?" He reaffirmed that he would. I said, "it's a good thing that the girl you ran a train on didn't have a brother like you, because if she did, you would have gotten your butt kicked, now wouldn't you?" The only way to describe the look on his face as he recognized that I had totally set him up and that what he had actually done was dumb, was priceless. As the other students in the class picked up on what I had just done, their response was also priceless. Note: I have no idea where I got that from. It was off the top of my head.

This young man then hung his head in shame. Now that I had him in a position of submission, I could have easily continued to belittle him and embarrass him more in front of his peers. I chose to shift gears and focus on the entire group of boys. I knew that he was not the only one abusing females. It's just that he was the only one who was bold enough to expose himself to everyone. I then shifted gears to the entire class. I explained to everyone how I have five fine sisters, how they can all take care of themselves, and they are all beautiful. But I'm always keeping an eye out for the opposite sex. Why? Because I know exactly what and how they think and what the opposite sex wants. It just so happens to be the exact same thing that I want and that I am looking for as well. I made it clear to each of them that I would hurt anybody who would hurt one of my family members, period. I also told them that I keep this in the forefront of my mind when I am dealing with females. So, I reminded each of them that when they are dealing with a female, that person is somebody's sister, daughter, aunt, child, mother, etc. I also said, what goes around, comes around. When you disrespect someone else's female family member, somebody can and will disrespect yours. That young man in the class who got totally embarrassed, later came to me and thanked me for that graphic picture that I painted for him. It really hit home. It really helped him put things in perspective. I told him, "no problem. That is why I'm here." I am fully aware that for many of the young men's view of women is very abstract. And until the view is changed, the way they see women will remain objective, sorely lacking and forever wanting.

Group Session 4: You Can't Give What You Don't Have

Forgive me, I have got to take this perspective and view of women to another level. I don't have any other choice in the matter. When it comes to young men, to recognize that they are lacking in a particular area is for the most part a good thing. Nevertheless, if they don't possess the tools to fix it or have access, they are still in trouble. Big trouble. This is one of those areas where I tried, I really tried, but I always felt like it seemed to come up just a little bit short. It seemed that every time we had to leave this topic of woman, there was always some more that needed to be said or shared. Oh well. Below is a continuation of what I said earlier about the view and perspective of women, but this takes it to another level. It takes it to a level that some of us won't go and others can't go. Regardless, it is still a losing proposition, if they aren't willing to first look at themselves.

On too many occasions, I would reiterate to the young men that their personal respect was more important than their very life. They would rather die, than be disrespected and many have. Unfortunately, all too many of them didn't recognize how deeply this issue of self-disrespect had been woven within their lives on a daily basis.

The young men were running around demanding respect. And when respect wasn't given, it appeared that all hell broke loose. Here's when it really got crazy. What good was gaining respectful desires, when you didn't know how to love yourself to begin with? Many haven't figured out how to avoid returning to the facility, which equals freedom, in their quest to be respected. But nevertheless, they were willing to do additional time, even if they were embarrassed in front of their peers.

When I looked to the kids' future as potential adults, fathers and husbands, a weight came over me. Where were they going to gain the necessary tools to acquire the proper insight to carry on a viable relationship with anybody, let alone a woman? The foundation for any healthy relationship starts with self-love; with self-respect; and self-esteem. When had anyone sat down with them or spent time with them on these critical issues?

<u>Group Session 5: Excuse Me. I'm Not Invisible.</u>

With too many of the young men, if you looked at them the wrong way or they thought you were trying to embarrass or intimidate them, they would step to you in a second. It didn't matter who you were or where you were from or even if you were carrying a gun. Their respect was more important than even their own lives. And too many of them had lost their mobility, their bustling future, and some, even their lives because of that all-important need for ultimate respect. Knowing that this thing called respect for many was a matter of life and death, I shared the following true story.

Since no one wants to be disrespected, not even me, I was compelled to share the following true story with them about my own personal experience. I wanted them to have a real-life example of how with the right tools and right perspective, you can turn a potentially volatile situation into a very smooth transition. And, with the right finesse, make it a win-win. After I retired from the Army and was visiting in Baltimore, Eddie Murphy had just come out with the first, Nutty Professor movie. I openly volunteered to pay for my family and nephew's family to go and see it. Altogether it was seven of us. The show we attended had a long line and it was very hot. I told my family to wait near the door, out of the sun, while I waited in line to purchase the tickets. The wait to reach the ticket clerk was about twenty-five minutes. With two people in front of me to go, things got a little crazy. The young man who was two people in front of me paid for his tickets, but they were the incorrect tickets. He discovered this when he tried to go into the actual theater where the movie was showing. In the meantime, the woman right in front of me, appeared to get the right tickets. As she collected her tickets and moved to enter the theater, the previous young man returned and without a word to me, stepped right in front of me and began to yell at the clerk who sold him the incorrect tickets. Anybody witnessing this - my family, other patrons' or bystanders, might have gotten the wrong impression that this guy was jumping the line. And since he was very loud and abrupt as he approached the clerk, all eyes were on the ticket counter and the clerk. I personally felt that this young man had not only embarrassed me in front of others, he embarrassed me in front of my family. What would they think of me? What were they thinking about me, under these circumstances? Am I just going to stand there and let this guy disrespect me? So, under these conditions, I felt that I had a couple of options. I chose the following avenue to deal with this conflict. As I heard him yelling at the clerk, when I saw him take a breath, I then said, "excuse me sir?" He turned and before I could say another word, he began to tell me why he was yelling at the clerk and how him disrespecting me was merely a by-product of the clerk's incompetence and was not intentional. I then said, "That's all fine and good sir, but I'm not invisible." He immediately grasped my intent, calmed down and started apologizing. I then told him not to worry about that. I told him, they made a mistake and to go on and get his tickets taken care of and he did. Afterwards, I bought my tickets and took my family into the movie as if nothing had happened, and we all had a wonderful time.

But this situation did not have to turn out the way that it did. This young man obviously disrespected me and made me look pretty lame and foolish in front of my family, friends and strangers. I had every right to be angry and wanted to do something about it. But instead of being reactive, I chose to be proactive. In the same instant the offense occurred to me, I tried to find a way to address the disrespect, while giving him a chance to check himself and it worked. I chose to make it a win-win. At the moment I said, "But,

I'm not invisible," he realized on his own that he had crossed a line that he should not have. I was able to accomplish this without me retaliating or trying to embarrass him, in the meantime. I believe that at that moment, he recognized his error and the situation he had placed me in, simultaneously. I also believe his acknowledgement through the apology allowed me the liberty to let him go ahead and finish the process anyway, without future embarrassment to me or to himself. Yet, things did not have to turn out this way. He could have had a gun. He could have had some other friends jump me. He could have swung on me or hit me. He could have waited until the movie was over and then confronted me. A number of other ugly things could have happened at that moment, but it didn't. Would I do what I did here, in the future? You bet. What he did was wrong and I believe that it needed to be addressed and being afraid of the possible consequences didn't and wouldn't stop me from doing the right thing. But I wasn't crazy either. I wanted the kids to see that this was a very serious matter, and how using my head, instead of my emotions, benefited all parties involved. You have got to choose your battles. I told the kids that everyone's objective is to win the war but in order to win the war of life, you must fight some smaller battles. You cannot and will not win all of the battles. Nevertheless, if you win enough small battles, you have a much better chance of winning the overall war. I wanted them to realize that sometimes silence and restraint in a matter are not signs of weakness, but in-turn, signs of strength. In addition, this openly demonstrated that I had more than one tool in my tool box. The true essence of the program and reaching out to the kids was to help them find a way to build, assess, acquire, and recognize what tools they had in their tool boxes. I just hoped that real-life stories like that one, could reach them to help them see that if they don't have these types of tools in their tool-box, it could prove to be very costly. It could even cost them their lives. That's why I was there to help them.

Nevertheless, after the movie was over and I dropped off my nephew and his family, I told my wife that I needed to leave Baltimore. She asked why? I said because somebody will probably kill me. See, I'm not afraid to confront that which I believe is wrong and I'm not afraid of the consequences that go with confrontation. I am one of those people who believes that evil can only prosper, when good men keep silent. Notwithstanding, I also know that some people in these streets, don't care if I show them respect, give them a way to escape or just keep my mouth shut. Good man or not, they will hurt me and, in some cases, even take my life. I am very self-aware that my self-control alone, under every circumstance is not going to save me from a diminished confrontation, with someone lacking the right tools. Some people just don't care, period. It is what it is. I call this optimism, with a taste of realism. You've got to check yourself, before you wreck yourself.

### Group Session 6: America's Got Talent? I've Got Talent Too.

If you let them tell it, each of the young men was going to be the next, Michael Jackson, Jay-Z, Naz, P-Diddy, etc. To prove that they had what it takes, they would at the drop of a hat be ready to rap or rhyme. So, if you prompted them, they were ready to perform for you on the spot. Now, here is the real sad part of all of this. My fellow staff members were basically telling them that pursuing a musical career was simply a waste of time and unrealistic. Without any encouragement, the staff would just cut them to the bone about the entertainment industry, but wouldn't give them the other side. On the other hand, I was trying to stir up inside of the kids the ability to dream again, while many of my fellow staff were saying to them that it was stupid and they were wasting their time. Although most of the kids were not going to make it, being a dream-stealer was not the best road to take, considering the young men's situation. If you are going to take something, then give them something. Give them anything, but don't give them nothing.

I personally tried to take a more balanced approach as I addressed this subject. When a kid told me he wanted to be the next rapper or go into hip-hop, the following is how I usually handled it. My first response would be something like, "great, fantastic, I'm scared of you." This would usually catch them off-guard. Seeing that the first thing they expected to hear was negative. In addition, I would say this, "You know that <1% of those in the entertainment industry make it to the big time; but guess what? You could be in that <1%. Don't forget, it isn't that you plan to fail, you failed to plan. And make sure that you have a backup plan. Make sure that you are academically competent. What good is hiring a lawyer to write you a contract that you can't read? And how do you know that the mathematical percentage that is being negotiated for you by your agent is worth the paper that it is written on? Be honest and realistic about making it out there. But don't quit just because the odds are against you. Nothing beats a failure but a try." For so many, doing rap and hip-hop is a step up from their previous behavior. So, for many of the kids they had replaced their old dreams with new dreams. There was no way I was going to snatch away their dreams and hopes, because at least they were dreaming. At least they were hoping once again.

<u>Group Session 7: Let's Talk About Some Real Money</u>

Since I know how important music is to most of them, I decided to do something very special for the kids. I brought in some music videos from all walks of life to show them that there is more to the music industry than the performing and writing song-raps. I talked to them about how many of these artists were also producers, owned their own studios, labels and collaborated with and wrote for other artists. I showed them that there was more to the music than the words that rhyme. I talked to them about how a group like TLC made millions of dollars for their record label, but the performers themselves got peanuts. I then shifted gears and said that being just a rapper or performer was not enough these days. If you want to make it big in the entertainment industry, you've got to get in front of the mic. You should be looking for multiple streams of income. You should be positioning yourself to learn, grow and expand your name and your game. Then I made a statement that caught some of them off guard. "I don't want to be like Mike. He doesn't make enough money for me. I want to be like the owner of the Bulls." I went on to say that if the owner of the Bull is paying Michael Jordan $19-million dollars a year, don't you think the owner is making just a little bit more? I then told them that this is why I am not impressed with Michael Jordan's financial position, because there is far more money to be made elsewhere. Speaking of elsewhere - please don't get it twisted. I am not trying to disrespect Michael Jordan. In order for him to be making $19-million dollars a year, he had to pay his dues. Guess what? We all have to pay our dues. If you look into Mr. Jordan's past, the one thing you won't see are short-cuts and excuses. When he got cut, when he was told that he wasn't good enough, it just made him work harder. Michael Jordan became so excellent at his craft that you are forced to watch him, no matter what. He compelled us to admire his greatness. He didn't ask or beg you to watch him perform, you just did. The expression is written all over your face after his performance. Those who reach this pinnacle in life get to write their own ticket. And, Michael Jordan was no different. Nevertheless, with all of this on his side, there were still limitations. If certain things were not in place and paid for ahead of time, we the public would never have gotten to know who the real Michael Jordan is.

So, with that said, you have got to go to school, get a job, and do well at whatever employment you have. All of us are not going to make it to the NBA, NFL, etc. So, get a job and do well at it. But always work yourself out of a job. Why? No one is ever going to pay you what you are worth, but you. The diploma or degree gets your foot in the door. But once you get inside, then you have to prove your worth.

For some of us that worth is a steady paycheck. For some of us that means raises and advancement within and/or outside of the company. Then for some of us, each job or place of employment is nothing more than a stepping stone or platform for the next level. For those of you who understand your true worth, that ultimate level is always reaching for self-employment or being a business owner.

When you don't have ownership or part ownership, you are building someone else's dream. When you have ownership or part ownership, then you are building your own dream. Wishing, hoping, thinking, will not make ownership come to pass. You have to have a game plan. It needs to be in place and you're working on it. You can't be sitting around waiting for someone to just give it to you. See, gimme got his neck broke, by his kinfolk. I hear you loud and clear telling me what you want, but I don't see you taking the necessary steps to make it come to pass. I can tell that you mean well, but your actions are speaking so loudly that I can't hear a word you are saying. You can make money and you can make excuses, but you don't have time to make both. The choice is yours. Think about it?

### Group Session 8: The $100,000 Dollar Drug Dealer

I estimated that between 75-85% of the kids either have sold drugs or know someone who they are associated with or hang with who sells drugs. Drugs are a big deal to most of these kids. I also believe that most of them smoke or have smoked weed before. Because of the huge potential for making a lot of money, I can see why a lot of them gravitate to the life of selling or using drugs. This is the particular lifestyle that I grew up around and has touched me and my family personally, from using to selling.

I've learned that no matter what end of the spectrum you find yourself on, it still gets pretty ugly. I didn't want to glamorize the drug trade, but I also wanted the kids to see that there were some parts of this puzzle that they were probably missing. I also wanted them to see that the odds weren't in their favor if they chose to stay in this arena. So, I asked the class a very important question. "How many of you in this classroom know a drug dealer who made at least $100,000 dollars last year? Not one kid ever raised their hand. I then said, "Don't get me wrong, there are drug dealers who made $100,000 dollars last year. It's just that you don't know any of them." With this proclamation out of the way, I knew that we could now talk honestly about drugs and selling drugs as it pertained to them and their future.

By using myself, I went on the chalkboard to show them how they were selling themselves short with their involvement in the drug trade. I first asked the students whether or not I appeared to be better off than them? They replied no. I asked the kids did they believe that I came from the same background that many of them come from? They all agreed. Once we all agreed that both they and I are on the same level, I proceeded to do the following. I wrote my name on the board and then proceeded to list all the present and pertinent amounts of income that I was receiving. I listed my retirement check, facility check, 2 part-time jobs, my per-diem paid as a full-time student and the amount the military paid for my full-time education. When I summed up all of the financial amounts, it came to more than $100,000 dollars, yearly. I made it clear to each person that this was not done to impress them or to belittle them. I made it clear that this was all legally obtained income. I didn't have to worry about the police or the Feds. I also didn't have to worry about getting shot by some other dude who wanted my corner or spot. I told the kids that, "if I come from the same background as you and I am no better than you and you are no better than me, here is more than $100,000 worth of income that I earned legally and from hard work. If I am no better than you and I have proven that it can be done, what is keeping you from achieving the same thing?" I then took the lesson to another level. I shared the following nugget with them. Some people call you a drug dealer. I call you an entrepreneur. You are running your own business. You know the cost of your product and how to divide it and stretch it to get maximum profit. You know who to give a discount or a free sample too. You also know when to charge more, based on demand. You know the streets and your clients. If you get busted, the real smart ones know how to not lose all of your product and money. Being an entrepreneur is smart and to stay an entrepreneur is smart. You just need a different vehicle to make that money. I told them that with a little hustle and due-diligence, they could find those other vehicles. The lack of positive role-models in the kids' lives is a real problem. Nevertheless, that doesn't mean that you get to use it as an excuse. Suck it up and keep it moving.

Group Session 9: Silicon Valley vs. Silicon Alley

Some of the kids say they won't work at McDonald's or Burger King. I told them that I'll work at a fast-food joint in a minute, if it means that's what I have to do in order to support and take care of my family. Because taking care of my family and myself is paramount. I can't see my involvement in any activities that could get me locked up or even killed as being a benefit. So, anything that is involved with drugs is a no-go. I told them that low paying jobs are nothing more than stepping stones to reach those high paying jobs. I believe that too many of them try to take short-cuts, because there is nobody present in their lives to show them another way other than the illegal or under the table schemes to succeed.

I purposely and willfully choose not to allow what I strive for and what I do, to define who I am. I also believe that if the work I do is honest work, I should have no problem performing it, no matter what that job is. Yet, a number of the kids feel that minimum wage and fast food jobs were beneath them. I wanted the kids to see that everything they saw on the surface, might not be all that was there in a given situation. And I also wanted them to know that doing their homework and due diligence could prove to be very profitable. I asked if any of them ever played a little pick up ball in their neighborhoods, when they lived in NYC. They affirmed that they did. I then said, if a stranger asked for the next game are you going to just let them win or are they going to have to come in, work hard and earn a win? They would have to earn it. Usually the home team won't lose or give up until they want to. Strangers aren't going to just walk in and take over. Nevertheless, the best of the strangers have already done their homework before they even ask for the next game. They have sized up the competition; checked out the strength and weaknesses and then used that to their advantage when the game started. When the outsiders win, usually the home team will give them their props, because they won it fair and square. But seldom will a stranger just walk on the court without giving the proper respect to the guys that are from that neighborhood like they own the court. It's called courtesy. It's called respect.

When I shared this story about an outsider needing to show at least some respect, because if they won, they seldom had any beef with the normal homeboys. Then I made a statement and I asked a question that kind of threw some of them off. I said that most of you can't see yourselves working in McDonald's, Burger King or for minimum wage, right? Most of the kids affirmed my suspicions. I then asked how many of them have ever heard of Silicon Valley? Only one kid's hand went up and all he knew was it was in

California. I went on to ask them had anyone heard of Silicon Alley? Not one of them knew that it was in NYC, right off of Wall St. I went on to tell the kids how during the Dot-Com bust many internet companies were formulated and put on the stock market for sale at $10-20 a share out in Silicon Valley. Those who got in at the beginning or behind the cycle were given thousands of individual stocks and/or an opportunity to purchase more at that same low rate. It was nothing for an individual to have 5,000-10,000 shares of stock in these new companies. I told them that based on projected growth, earnings, business model and projected profits, many of these companies soared in the market from $10 a share to anywhere from $250-$400 a share, when the company went public. Now think about the person behind the scenes who was given or purchased their stocks for next to nothing, just became an instant millionaire and hadn't done anything, but just being in on the beginning of a good deal that paid off. This exercise went on for about three years. In the meantime, Silicon Alley also, which is right off of Wall Street in NYC got in on the same fray. It followed the same pattern as Silicon Valley in California. People got rich overnight. The kids were shocked to know that this place existed in their own backyard and they didn't have a clue that millions of dollars were instantly being made there. Unfortunately, I knew this, but they didn't.

I made it clear to each of the kids that this boom only lasted for about three years and then the bottom fell out. But that wasn't the point. I went back to the example of the pick-up game and a stranger coming in from out of town or somewhere else. I told them that I'm not from NYC, but I know about Silicon Alley and its lucrative financial connections. I then went on to say that minimum wage and fast food jobs are not beneath me. If I lived in NYC, I would have been down there in Silicon Alley, washing cars, running errands, sweeping and taking out the trash, getting somebody's lunch. All I'm looking for is someone to give me a chance. I told these young men that after I had proven myself to be loyal and hardworking at the menial things, I won't have to worry about asking a good businessman for a raise or step up. He will offer it to me himself. A good businessman is always on the lookout for hard workers. I assured the guys that by six months, I would have gone from the outside or the runner to at least working inside. And who knows within a year, maybe even become an Intern. But that's not going to happen if I'm not in school. That's not going to happen if I'm always in trouble with the law or locked up. That's not going to happen if I think that menial jobs are beneath me. I have to be hungry. There has to be a fire inside of me that won't quit no matter what. I have to be willing to do whatever the next guy won't do.

I had to make it clear as I was telling this story to them that I am the outsider. Nevertheless, I have come to their home turf and spied out a very lucrative financial deal that they didn't have a clue existed. How are you going to let an outsider come in and get an advantage that you don't have? You are not handling your business. I didn't want to shame these guys as much as I wanted them to see that at times their closed-mindedness about menial labor was selling them short when it came to future profitable possibilities. I think most of them got the gist of where I was coming from. I also told them that this Dot-Com craze was just another fad and a lot of people in the long run got hurt. But the smart ones flipped their money right after the stock shot up, took out their money, and put it in other instruments. Moral of the story - It's for the needy and not the greedy. They knew how to diversify. They knew how to put their eggs in more than one basket.

# VOLUME IV

# Finding The Missing Pieces, Nugget By Nugget

# FIXING THE BROKEN

**WITHOUT BEING BROKEN**

TURNING ON THE LIGHT, SO THAT CHANGE CAN TAKE PLACE

## JEROME REDD

# Nugget 1: The Drug Life Vs. The Thug Life

For most of these kids, their role models are in the entertainment industry, sports figures or drug dealers. Bottom-line, these folks bring home a lot of money and they've got juice. When you've got money and respect, nothing else matters. On the flip side, I tried to get them to recognize that the ability to achieve these accolades can and usually does come at a great price. Everybody does not have it and some don't know how to possess what it takes to beat that less than one percent success rate.

As I listened to their stories about how they grew up, it became apparent how they were trapped in the quagmire. The only role-models in the home and neighborhood are the drug dealers and the only role-models outside the home are sports figures, entertainers and rappers. When it comes to their parents as workers or the drug-dealer, the drug-dealer seems to always catch their eyes more. So why work for a living? Why settle for low-paying, no-paying jobs, when it's much easier to become a drug dealer and there are no prerequisites or job requirements to join? The same thing applies if you want to be a gang member.

While growing up in Baltimore, I was faced with this same dilemma. Too many of the role-models in my life were negative. Nevertheless, I didn't choose the easy route. I didn't chase the fast money. I can only believe that it was a God-sent sixth-grade teacher, Mr. Posey, who made all the difference in my life. I just knew there was more, because he made me believe that there was more. And he was right.

I made one thing clear to all these kids. There are no short-cuts. You have to pay the cost, to be the boss. You have to pay your dues. I can empathize with your plight and your childhood. I can even understand how you got here, but that won't get you success. It's going to take your hard work and your abilities. Excuses and short-cuts only make the journey longer. So, when are you going to stop whining and complaining and get down to some real work on your plans, on your goals, your dreams, your life?

# Nugget 2: The Trust Factor

Every person you are affiliated with can't have your back. It can be family, friends, neighbors, associates, mentors or strangers. The people you are surrounded by, might mean well, but can they deliver? When times get tough and everything is hitting the fan, can you depend on them to step up? Understand something. In some cases, it isn't that they won't. They can't. They don't possess the basic skill-set to assist you under normal situations, let alone, a troubled one. If you are going to be honest with yourself and your future, there must be a selection process when it comes to those with whom you are affiliated and surrounded by. When I was a very young man, I heard this powerful speaker (Les Brown) say. "Surround yourself with quality people." Bad people attract bad people. Good people, attract good people. Are you getting the message?

You should always be working on yourself, but in-turn, always evaluating who you are associated with and allow into your corner and inner-circle. You can't just let anybody in. You can't trust everyone, especially when they haven't proven themselves to be trustworthy. So, while I'm working on myself, I'm also reaching out to those around me and making a cognitive assessment of where they are as it pertains to their impact on my life. This assessment pertains to both positive and negative impact.

This assessment also allows me to determine who stays and who goes, as I am moving through life. I make it a distinct point to determine both the strengths and weaknesses of those in my life There are certain people that you allow into your life, while others at times, are just thrust upon you. For example, there are folks like family, boss, teacher, neighbor, etc. who you just have to put up with. While there are others, you can pick and choose. I would advise that no matter which category they fall in, you need to size up both. Your future depends on it.

It is not your job, per se, to change those that are around you. Nevertheless, it is your job to determine whether or not, based on their strengths and weaknesses, if they can be of assistance to what you are trying to achieve. This challenge isn't just for those who are close to you. This challenge is for your superiors, subordinates, contemporaries, and others. Knowing what they can do and cannot do, can save you a lot of heartache and misery. If you are fully aware that someone isn't capable of handling a certain responsibility, then you won't be the least bit disappointed when they fail. Yet, because you already possess that knowledge, why would you depend on them to handle that task properly in the first place? You wouldn't. You would take the necessary actions to prevent such a catastrophe from ever happening. There will also be cases that are beyond your personal control. This could involve a parent, or a boss or someone in law enforcement. Let's say they are in a position to affect an outcome which is either for you or against you. You need to try as best you can to remove your own feelings and emotions in that matter, and observe and process the facts. When the time and circumstances are right, this situation can be revisited with the hope of a different outcome. But guess what? You have got to be patient. The reward will be worth it.

Know this. Everybody can't come with you and everybody will not have your back. While you are working on you, also start figuring out, who is going to help you reach your goals and who is not. As you are determining this, you need to also come up with a game plan to ensure that this works. You need people around you who will be constantly pushing and telling you the truth. If your feelings get hurt, oh well, you'll get over it. What you can't afford to have are those who are telling you what sounds good and only what you want to hear. I am a very strong, self-willed man who knows himself extremely well. Nevertheless, I have a few people in my life who can stop me in the middle of a sentence and I will listen to every word they have to say to me. Why? Because I trust them. Because they are always pouring into me, what is best for me, period. Trusting the right people will save your future. Trusting the right people will save your life.

# Nugget 3: I Guess You Can Call Me A Poet. But At The Times, I Didn't Know It.

While working at the facility, there were two separate times when one of the kids lost a relative. In one case, the kid lost a cousin and in the other case the kid lost his grandmother. Both of the kids requested that they be afforded the opportunity to be escorted home to attend the funeral. In both cases the young men were denied. And although, I was unaware of why they were denied, I could clearly see that these deaths were taking a toll on both of the kids. Now here's where I stepped in. Because I write poetry, I decided to offer to write a poem for each of the young men's family members.

Volunteering for this task, in my opinion, was no big deal. I asked each of these young men to tell me a little bit about this particular relative and I would in turn write them a poem. To my amazement, they were both extremely flattered and pleased with what I had written. In both of these cases, I didn't make any fanfare or stir about what I was doing. None of the kids or the staff knew what I had done. Notwithstanding, it didn't take long before my attributes became the talk of the town.

Since writing poetry has always been and still is a very private thing, I just kind of blew off all the nice attention and focused back on the kids and the program. And, although that was good enough for me, I learned very quickly that the kids weren't satisfied with my shy humility. So, one day I was asked would I be willing to bring in some of my poetry and share it with them? Reluctantly, I said yes.

On this auspicious day, I brought in about 5-10 poems that I figured they might like. These were my more hip-hop poems. To my amazement, I was utterly wrong. They loved my poetry. And, what they had to say next, only knocked me to my knees. One of the kids asked if I was published. I responded with no. I told him that I just do this for fun. More than one of the kids told me that I was good enough to be published. Knowing that the kids took rapping and rhyming seriously, there was something to what they are telling me. I didn't learn until years later that they were right on the money, after I successfully published three books of poetry. I also realized that my ability to step out on faith and get this accomplished was directly related to these kids. I also addressed these turn of events, in Book 3. The Poetic Journey.

# Chapter 17
# The Last Shall Be First

During the weekdays at the facility, the whole day was basically structured until homework time at 9pm. However, on the weekends, many of the activities are geared towards the enjoyment and relaxation of the kids. One of the activities on Sundays was the religious time. Due to the way I carried myself and spoke, many of the young people and even the staff knew that I was a Christian. I didn't flaunt my beliefs, but neither did I hide them under a bushel. Nevertheless, I was on point and I was understood. I understood from my past military days that if I wasn't careful, my religious beliefs could possibly become a conflict of interest. One of the things that I really worked hard at, was to ensure that no one, kid or staff, would accuse me of trying to proselytize them. I knew that some of the staff were already accusing me of being too soft when it came to physically restraining a kid. If I had talked to folks about being a Christian, I believe that that would only make it worse for me overall. I also believed that if the light of God is within you, it will come out anyway and it cannot be hidden; even if you try and believe me, I tried.

One of the nice things that happened to me at the facility was I got to bid on what we called the "Weekend Warrior" shift and I got it.

On this shift you got to work 16 hours on Saturday, 16 hours on Sunday, and 8 hours on Monday. That was your 40-hour week. Obtaining this shift allowed me the ability to return to college as a full-time student, during the week. I was a very happy camper.

In the meantime, the Chaplain who was handling religious time on Sundays, stopped. No one stepped up or took his place. And, although the facility kept religious time on the schedule, we just let the kids, play games, read and write letters, etc. Some of the kids weren't satisfied with this arrangement and started to complain. Then some of them approached me and asked if I would conduct religious time with them on Sundays. They realized my schedule fit because of the Weekend-Warrior shift, and they trusted me. Of course, I was flattered. But I made it very clear to them that the State was not paying me to conduct religious time. It was paying me to be a staff member in the facility. I also knew that in the eyes of some, I was not their favorite staff. If they would have perceived this as being beneficial to the kids, they would have blocked it. The benefit to the kids didn't matter to some staff. Now tell me that ain't sad?. What I knew and believed were the following. And, I shared it with the kids. If I bring this up to the leadership, I believe that it will get shot down immediately. Knowing I was not one of their favorite staff, a request of this nature would only make things worse for me. That meant there was only one way the leadership would buy into or consider this request. I then told the kids that if it was what they really wanted, I didn't have a problem with conducting it. But, they were going to have to convince the leadership that they wanted me. If so, then the leadership might agree to allow it. Otherwise, I was just going to keep on doing my everyday job, three days a week and go on about my business.

Based on the atmosphere at the facility and how certain folks in leadership positions didn't like me, I thought this was going to be a dead deal. I was totally wrong. At my local church, I briefly spoke to my Pastor about this request. I believed he would rather have me in church on Sunday, than somewhere else. Therefore, I wanted his permission. I also told him how nice it would be if this could happen for the kids' sake, being they asked for me specifically, but I didn't think it would happen. Yet, he gave me his blessing anyway.

To my utter surprise, the facility came back with a yes to the request. At first I thought to myself, this could be just what they are looking for to hang me. All they needed was one kid or one of the staff complaining that I was trying to proselytize someone and I would be done. Nevertheless, I went on to prove that this could possibly be a gain for the sake of the kids, and far out-weighed any harm or inconvenience that could happen to me surrounding this decision. So, I stepped up cautiously and I moved forward in this matter.

With the approval, the leadership then approached me about the kid's request. I made it clear that I didn't mind, but it was not my idea and that I would be happy performing my regular job along with this additional responsibility. I was then told that it was okay to conduct the religious time as long as it didn't interfere with program. If there was a problem, like a restraint or lack of staff, etc., there would be no religious time. I said I understood this and welcomed it. I said that it made perfect sense to do it this way.

Okay, I'm now in charge of religious time, but I have never conducted religious time in a correctional facility before. What am I supposed to do? Good question. The answer to the question turned out to be very simple and a biblical one. Treat the kids the same way you would like to be treated if it were you here sitting in those seats. The classroom held 20 chairs for students. Since I knew the kids held different beliefs, , here are some of the rules that I implemented.

    a. We will respect differences. Everybody doesn't believe what you believe. Just because someone believes differently than you, doesn't make it right or wrong. When you give respect, you get respect.

    b. There will be no gang-signs or gang-related affiliation in this group. The first time I see it, you are done. You are out of here. I'm not having it.

c. This is your religious time not my religious time. I am a facilitator. I am not your Pastor, your Priest or your Rabbi. I am here to assist you, and not to proselytize you.

Laying out ground rules in any situation is critical, to reduce conflict and chaos. I knew I had to reach the kids where they were. Yet conveyed that I wasn't just another staff teaching religious time. I was believing that this opportunity was a calling to make a difference on a spiritual level. So, in speaking to the kids, I shared the following. "I know that some of you are going to have questions that you are going to ask me and that is okay. But let me make something perfectly clear up front. I am a Christian and my authority for what I have to say to you and how I live comes from the Word of God, the Bible." (And I held up my Bible for each kid to see). "When you ask me a question, I will not be giving you my opinion. I will be giving you what is in, "Thus Saith the Lord". I trust His Words more than my very thoughts." I then went on to tell them that every week I would bring them a lesson plan (And I held up the lesson plan. I then held up the Bible also and made the following statement.). "The lesson plan is optional, but for me, the Word of God is never optional." So, when you ask me a question, my answer/s will come from the Word of God and not what I think. This was the only non-negotiable parameter I had for the group. I had no clue how powerful that proclamation would be by the time I stepped down two years later from facilitating their religious time.

Was the religious time a success? You better believe it. I got to do this for about two years before a new Chaplain came on board. My initial group started out with about 5 kids. By the time I stopped doing religious time, I had to turn kids away from the classroom. My class could only hold 20 students at a time. It turned out that the more I tried to be quiet and let them share, the more they would ask me faith-based questions. The more they asked me questions, the more I got to share the Word of God with them. That's when I realized what had happened, and I was blown away. Because I purposely went out of my way to assure them and others that I wanted to honor their religious time and not put Christianity first, that is exactly what happened. I went out of my way to try to get the young men to communicate with each other on topics and issues, but they instead kept asking me for my opinion. I kept giving them Scripture. So, the more I tried not to put God first out of respect for them, God ended up being brought to the forefront, anyway. Wow!

When the new Chaplain finally came on board, the young men didn't like him and requested that I continue doing the religious time. I was compelled and flattered, but I had to remind them of the circumstances under which I acquired the additional duty in the first place. We now have a new Chaplain. I must now return to my normal duties. The duties that I was being paid for. I made it perfectly clear that the powers-that-be were not going to let me remain in this wonderful lap of luxury, and they didn't.

Now that the years have passed and I have had time to reflect and think back, I consider what took place for those two years, was nothing less than a miracle. There is no way that I could have imagined that what happened was going to happen. All I wanted to do was help out and make myself available. Nevertheless, every Sunday I was giving God's Word in detail and with authority. I could tell that the kids trusted me and they in turn, trusted what I had to say. And, I made it clear that I wasn't speaking for me. I was speaking for God and from God's Word. Hallelujah! Hallelujah!

# Nugget 4: How Does Freedom Really Taste

Since one shift included eight hours, they had to give us a lunch break, while we were watching the kids. The staff was given the option of eating what the kids ate or bringing their own meal with them. Since my wife is an excellent cook, I chose to bring my meals with me.

I quickly noticed that my daily meals were anticipated and the topic of discussion with the kids. I would wait until all of the kids had their meal and were eating and while the other staff watched, I heated up my meal. Upon return, the other staff would do likewise. The aroma from my meal would fill the entire mess hall and surrounding room. I told you, my wife is a great cook. On occasion, a kid would comment on the food I bought. Their conversation might go something like this. "Sergeant Redd, that food sure smells good." I would then take a bite and reply with the following. "It tastes good too."

And I would keep right on eating until I was finished. Some might say and some did say that was cold. My reply would be that I meant for it to be cold. An hour later, while in class, I would bring up the incident in the mess hall from earlier. I would ask them how they felt about what I said and how cold it sounded. Some would make it very clear that they didn't think what I did was cool. I would then remind them that because I have choices, because I'm free, I can eat their food or my food too. The answer I chose is a no brainer. I felt compelled to remind them of what a bad choice can do and deny you of.

Just in case they weren't listening, I shared the following. " When you return to NYC and you are out there all by yourself and it's 3am in morning or you and your boys are about to do something very, very stupid, I want you to remember this moment and this place right now. Once your freedom is taken away, you have to listen to somebody else. Somebody else telling you when to get up and when to go to bed. Someone else telling you when to eat and what to eat. Someone else telling you when you can go home or how long you stay. When you make dumb decisions, you give away your rights."

# Chapter 18
## The Thought For Today

When I first started working at the facility, my shift was usually 3-11pm. There was very little down time, if any. After we put the kids to bed around 9:30pm, we used the rest of the time to finish our paperwork. When the next shift came on, we would head for home, unless someone didn't show up for their shift.

I didn't like the grave-yard or the overnight shift. It went from 11pm-7am. By the time I got the kids up at 6am and they got dressed and went to the mess hall, it was time to change shifts. So, overnight, I didn't get to spend any quality time with them. This really irritated me and I figured that I would just have to live with this when it happened. I also knew that I didn't want to volunteer for overtime on the night-shift or to bid for that shift.

Then one night something miraculous happened. I had to go back and forth between the advanced team and the basic team, because I moved from one team to the other on the overtime shift. What I noticed as I kept passing through the mess hall was that there was some information written on the chalkboard. Then it hit me. Every kid in this facility has to go through the mess hall three times a day, morning, noon, and evening. Since I only have a brief moment with them in the mornings, when I'm on the overnight shift,

I could leave them a message on the board in the morning. I called it "The Thought for Today." From that day forward, at around 2-4am when no one was around, I would go down to the mess hall and put a message on the chalkboard for the kids.

When I started this trend, to be very honest, I was just being selfish. Realizing that I was only able to spend less than an hour with them on that shift, I was determined to leave them something I knew could last until I returned at 3pm. Guess what? I was right. I learned later that during academic classes and MAGIC, the comments written on the chalkboard would from time to time come up in discussion. But it didn't stop there. Because I kept this a secret from everyone, it later became an issue as to who was the culprit who started this trend within the facility. And of course, my lips were sealed. In Books 2 and 3, I will talk a little more about the odd circumstances surrounding this ordeal. I will also talk about how I turned a negative, into a positive. In the meantime, below are just a few of those messages I left on the board, to give you a taste. You will find the complete listing in Book 3, The Poetic Journey.

# THE THOUGHT FOR TODAY

1. Don't count the days, make the days count.
2. If life is an open book, what of value will the world find written on your pages.
3. If you don't have something worth standing up for, you will fall for anything.
4. Aspire to go higher. If you just put your mind to it, you can set the world on fire. Got a match?
5. True greatness isn't measured in the words you profess, but are demonstrated in the values you possess.
6. Aspire to greatness. Today's youth would do better, If they knew better.
7. You can do anything you put your mind to. But don't forget, you've got to pay the cost, to be the boss.
8. Your greatest battles are fought and won in the mind, first.
9. It's OK to fight for what you believe in. Question: Do you really know what you believe in?
10. Before you can truly know someone else, you must first know yourself.

# Nugget 5: When to Call And When Not to Call

The rules of engagement were very clear. Once the kids left the facility, I had no means to stay in touch with them. I couldn't visit them, reach out to them, or contact them. The kids that went to our aftercare, could and did reach out to me from time to time at the facility only. My relationship with them was strictly facility-related. And although, I didn't like this policy or procedure, I clearly understood its meaning and purpose. I had much respect for this policy. Nevertheless, I knew that I was unorthodox, unconventional and a stretcher of the rules. For example:

1. I might write a phone number on the black board, without any name. Then I might have a conversation that went something like this. "For some strange reason these ten digits just popped into my head. If you feel compelled to write them down in your book with your other notes, that is strictly your business."

2. Then I would completely change the subject, which appeared to have nothing to do with the numbers I had written on the board. Then my conversation would go something like this. "Once you leave this facility, I personally cannot stay in touch with you or

reach out to you. But those same rules don't apply to you. If you desire or want to reach out to me, the system does not provide the same restrictions." I would then go on to mention how kids in the past had called me while they are at the after-care to tell me how they were doing. This is truly a blessing and inspirational.

    3. I would then say something to the kids who were truly paying attention and could see beyond what was on the surface. I would stand right next to my phone number and repeat the following.
" Some of you are ready to go home and some of you are not. And whether you are ready or not, some of you are still leaving. And I ain't mad at you. This is especially for those of you who are leaving soon. If it is 2am, 3am, in the morning or on Friday night, before you are about to do something stupid; before you do something that is going to get you locked up again, call me. I can't promise you that I will fix it, but I promise that I will do everything in my power to help. The city is about five hours from here, but I will be there with bells on." Now, there were those who missed it, and had that dumb look on their face while asking the question, "How are we going to call, we don't have your phone number." While, those who were paying attention, got it, had already written my number down and told the other kid, "He just wrote it on the board, but he didn't put his name with it." This way no one could ever accuse me of giving any kid my phone number directly.

4. Unfortunately, there was a sad part to this exercise which I got to personally experience. I would explain that reaching out to me is a choice. It is an individual choice and that choice isn't for everybody. I made this perfectly clear to every kid in the room. I was willing to let them wake me up out of my bed and leave my family to go to help them. "See, you're my future. But, if you ever get locked up at Rikers, don't call me." A couple of kids had that puzzled look on their faces and asked me why I had adopted that philosophy towards Rikers. In a nutshell, I shared the following. "When you get locked up and they take you to Rikers, that is where the big boys go. We're talking about adult prison now. We are not talking about a juvenile facility. Once you go to Rikers, you don't need to call me. You need to call a lawyer."

5. One evening while I was on duty around 7-8pm, I received a call from one of the kids who had been there previously. But he wasn't calling me from home or from after-care. He was calling me from Rikers. So, as I asked him questions about his arrest and listened to his explanations, my heart sank. Over the phone, I didn't believe that he was innocent of killing this other kid. And with tears in my eyes, I had to ask this contradictory question. "Why, out of all the people that you could have called, did you call me?" His reply was that there was no one else for him to call. After I hung up the phone, I immediately told the other staff that I needed a quick break.

I then went into the lunch area, which was empty, and cried like a baby. That was too much for me to handle. He had no one to turn to and the one he did turn to, couldn't help him. I didn't sleep well that night or for the next few days. I felt so impotent. I could not believe how prophetic that phone call was. But I will tell you this. It made me work harder with the kids that I had left.

# Chapter 19
# Don't Forget How to Dream

When I listened to the kids telling me their stories and a little bit about their background, I noticed that a pattern started to appear. I call it the blame-game. My daddy was never there for me. My mom is a crack-head. I lived in the projects. The cops are out to get me. Regardless, I knew that these were just convenient excuses to keep them from facing up to their responsibility and the reality of their own actions. So, one day I said to the class, I want to try something if you would allow me. I first drew a square box on the board and then I drew some diagonal lines inside of this. I then labeled it, "Comfort Zone." I told them that inside of this comfort zone is where we all would like to be. This box makes us happy. We don't have to stretch, think, work, or try. We can just lay back and let it flow. I then told them that if they really want to be successful, they are going to have to come out of their comfort zone. This means that you have to get uncomfortable. You have to do something different. You have to try the unknown. And, as I was writing on the board, I told them that I wanted to try something with them. I told them to close their eyes for a moment and think back. I said too many of you, now that you are older, have forgotten those dreams that you had when you were little kids. As I told them to close their eyes and think back to when they were 7, 8, and 9 years-old. I said, "Do you remember when you saw a fire truck roaring down the street and said you wanted to be a fireman? You saw a man in a white smock and you said that you wanted to be a doctor. You saw the man in the uniform and you wanted to be a policeman". While I was speaking about these different occupations, I was also writing them on the black board. When I turned around to finish talking to the kids, I noticed that at least three kids had tears running down their faces. I quickly realized that I had hit a nerve with some of them. They started to remember their dreams. I went on to explain to them that I suffered from the same thing, for years. I told them how I allowed society to dictate my present and my future aspirations. I also told them how a Chaplain at Fort Hood, Texas, changed my life.

I shared with them the story of Carl Brashear. He was the first Black Navy diver during a sad period of segregation in this country. On the surface, you might say that his goals weren't high or lofty. Yet, this was something he truly wanted and knew he could do. How do we know this? He wrote to the Department of the Navy over 100 times requesting permission to go to Diving School. They finally said yes. I rhetorically asked the kids. How many times would you have written to the Navy, five, ten, twenty-five times? I knew for me personally, I wouldn't have written more than ten times. I wanted them to know that I was no better than them. But, this man full of heart and guts, kept on pursuing his goal. And, once they said yes, they still treated him like a second-class citizen. They tried to do everything to keep him from passing the course. He took what they threw at him and still passed. He wasn't just any person. He was relentless. While on a dangerous mission, one of his legs was severed at the knee. Most folks would have taken their military disability and got out of the Navy. He not only stayed in the Navy, he stayed in as a Navy diver. Can you imagine what he had to do in order to prove to the Navy that he was still fit to be a diver? This is an amazing story of courage, honor and determination. He wouldn't let anything or anybody keep him from the goal he set his mind to do. He refused to let what others thought of him or tried to characterize him as, define who he was. Most of these kids had never heard of Carl Brashear. But they could relate to his story. They could relate to his background. They could identify with his struggle. I just wanted them to see that you should never stop fighting for your dreams. You can't afford to give up on your goals. You have got to fight until you have got nothing left to fight for.

  What is it that you want out of life and how bad do you want it? I told them that if they wanted to they could take back their dreams from wherever they left them or allow them to be their own again. When your dreams are gone, you usually replace them with anger and despair or a substitute. But, it is not the same. As a result, now you have no hope, no drive and no decent future to look forward to. Dreamers have hope and hope never quits. Don't forget to make time to dream again. As a result of this experience, I wrote a poem about this. I called it "Don't Forget How to Dream." It is in Book 3: A Seed Manifested.

# Nugget 6: How'd You Do That?

No one in the facility had to sit me down and explain to me the importance of time. You can't get it back and it is always moving. Failure to appropriately utilize it can only result in a sad commentary. I knew the significance of it and tried to always use it to my and the kids' advantage. I spoke earlier about doing program, which included MAGIC, life-skills training, physical fitness, doing homework and learning basic living skills. Some of these were regularly programmed and some of these were done on the fly. It really boiled down to who was running the shift.

Since I had concluded that I was reaching and changing more kids' lives with my approach rather than the facility's approach, I always looked for methods and opportunities to interject my approach. Not only did I look for these opportunities, but I became very good at this saying, "You need to get in, where you fit in." When I finished a facility-run program or class, I didn't ask for assistance or directions. I improvised. I chose to intervene and included whatever subject matter I thought was appropriate at that time. There is a saying that I learned in the Army that fit perfectly here. "It is easier to ask for forgiveness, than permission." And, the kids never complained about whatever subject I choose. I got so good at this that at times when the door was shut and someone in authority would enter the room. I would turn on a dime and immediately change the subject as if I was speaking about it all the time before they arrived. After about 5-10 minutes, that person in authority would leave, and I would return to the previous subject matter, without skipping a beat. The look on the kids face when I performed this was priceless. On a few occasions, a kid would ask me how in the world was I capable of doing that. My immediate answer was, "I don't know." But I would also say the following. "My care for your success when you leave here outweighs my concern about being caught. So, in turn, I had become very good at this technique."

# Nugget 7: You Know He's a White Boy, Right?

When I started this story, I talked about Paul being White and me being Black. I also said that the majority of the kids were minority and the majority of the staff Caucasian. I also said that this story isn't about Black or White unless you want it to be. And I still mean that. Something amazing and truly wonderful happened to these kids while they were locked up and as a result, some of them will never look at the thing called race the same way again.

After working at the facility for about four years a new staff came on board, who was Caucasian, and he and I clicked immediately. His name is Bo. He and I were both retired Army. He and I had what some would call today, a Bro-mance. Since most of these kids lived around minority kids, when they saw he and I interacting, it left a lot of them dumb-founded and speechless. The looks on their faces made it very clear that they didn't believe this was actually happening, but it was. To add insult to injury, when he and I noticed their uncomfortableness, we would crank it up and make it even worse. Bo would make comments like, "I've never seen a Black man play ball as bad as you." And I would just play it off, because I knew he was trying to push my buttons in front of the kids. At another time, when we were playing a board game, I might say, "You know you don't want none of this, White boy." These kids knew under normal circumstances these comments would be fighting words. But they knew we were joking. Yet, they were totally bewildered. Some might say that this was cold, but it was extremely necessary.

Some of the kids would catch me alone and ask me about my relationship with this White man. I knew that it made them uncomfortable and I didn't try to change that. I knew that making them uncomfortable was a valuable tool, if I was going to reach them. I told them the following.

"Many of you grow up in and around those whom you know and are familiar with. You don't dare come out of your comfort zone unless it is absolutely necessary. You are also willing to fight and die for a flag or a piece of concrete corner that isn't even yours or theirs". I went on to say to them, "This White man and I are extremely close. I'm closer to him than with even some of my own family members. Why? He and I have been all over the world. We know that if the balloon should go up that while I am in the fox-hole with him, he has got my back and vice-versa. What I am talking about is putting my life in his hands and he is putting his life in mine.

That is a powerful trust that transcends, both race and color. If your comrade-in-arms does what he or she is supposed to do, there is a very good chance that both of you will make it back home alive. The bottom-line is that when someone has your back like that, you don't care what others think of you, what others have to say about you or the color of their skin. Cause most of them really don't know how deep it goes. It goes deeper than blood."

Both Bo and I knew that trying to explain this to relatives and friends was next to impossible. It was not something that could be easily explained. It was something you just had to live with. I tried to explain it this way to the kids. I told them that Bo was only a visitor in my home, one time. I showed him the refrigerator and the bathroom. The next time he visited, the house was his, period. The bond and love between the two of us was unexplainable, but the kids also knew, it was for real. This showed them a side of life that many of them had never experienced. Bo and I were honored that we were chosen to live out this experience in front of the kids, each day we worked at this facility. Bo and I also talked about how great it would be if the kids could be reached before they ever came in contact with the criminal justice system. Because of our personal interaction and the way that he kept it 100 with these kids, Bo always got more respect from the kids than the other White staff. It was simply amazing.

# Nugget 8: Never Forget

God did not bless my wife and me with any biological children. Nevertheless, we were both fortunate to help assist with the development and growth of some of our kin-folk. While stationed at the facility, I had the pleasure of getting a 3-week visit from 2 nephews and nieces during the Summer. I also made it a point to schedule a visit for both groups at the facility.

The kids at the facility were teenagers and so were my relatives. They got to visit for about 3 hours and have lunch with them. I watched closely their interactions with one another and their conversations. When the visit was over and I returned my relatives home, they and I had a very interesting conversation. Here a few of the questions I asked.

a. What did you think of them?

b. Did they appear dangerous?

c. Did they appear abnormal?

d. Could you see yourself hanging out with them?

When all was said and done, they couldn't find anything out of the ordinary with the boys. I then concurred with their assessment and added this one comment. "The only thing different between you and them is that they made a mistake and got caught." Knowing that my background was no different than those of the boys, I constantly reminded them that the only difference between them and me was I never got caught. I was not exempt nor was I criminally free. I was just never charged and convicted.

I also believe that this mindset kept me humble. It kept me focused on the importance of what was at hand and what I actually held in my possession. I also knew that these kids' lives depended on how I handled this knowledge.

# Chapter 20
# No He Didn't. Yes He Did

When these kids reached Stage 4, they were supposed to have the tools needed and inner-resources to draw upon, when they returned to New York City. You can believe that I touched, reached, engaged and pushed some of them harder than they had ever been pushed in their lives. I made it perfectly clear to them that if I never saw them again, I wouldn't be disappointed. I was so bad that I threatened most of them by letting them know that if I ever saw them back at this facility again, they would not be a happy camper for the rest of their time here. So, on the one hand, I pushed and I pushed hard. But, on the other hand, I made sure that I cultivated, questioned, verified, inspired, mentored, taught, cried and loved them to their release date. Each kid knew that when I was on shift, I was on shift. They didn't get some of me; part of me or mini-me. They got all of me. I would constantly put up the mirror of life in front of each of them and ask them did they like what they saw? If they didn't like what they saw, I would ask them, "What are you going to do about it? I can't go to New York City with you, when you leave here." I also wasn't afraid to tell them, if I didn't like what I saw. But, I still let them figure it out. I didn't have to like it, but it was their life and their decision. I was compelled to give them the same respect that I wanted for my decisions. When I finished a shift, I had gotten to the point where I would question if I had given enough, reached inside them enough, was tough enough, so that each kid could stand on their own. And guess what? I didn't know how to do it any other way. If they weren't prepared for destiny, I knew that I would see them again and very soon. So, did I take this personally? You better believe I did. And, I had an ugly past to prove what the alternative could be. For most of these kids it was time to go home, whether they were ready or not.

When a young man reached stage 4, I could not say with certainty whether or not that young was ready to return to the Big Apple. What I was sure of was that each of them who sat under my tutelage got to go through my personal mental boot camp. One day as I was pressing a young man on leadership and accountability, he said the following, "You make my head hurt." I gladly replied with a thank you, because I knew that I was making a difference that worked.

Am I guilty of working harder than most staff? I would say yes. I had a vested interest in the outcome of these kids' success. Was I reaching the kids? I would say yes, again. Were the kids in turn, responding to me? I would have to again say, affirmative. And, in the process of reaching those kids, was I making a difference? You better believe it. It became very apparent to me that after one month went by, and then two and three months, these kids had not returned to the facility. Wow! I would periodically check with the Director and Assistant Director on certain kids at our city program just to get an update on their progress. In most cases, it was in the affirmative. The kids who were struggling or running into some difficulties were usually because of things and issues the kids had no control over. Here are a few examples:

    a. A young man was habitually late every morning in getting to his program in the city. He was threatened that if he kept coming in late, he would be sent back up-state. When the leadership finally investigated, they discovered that the reason he was late all the time was due to the fact that his mother was a crack-head. The young man was forced every morning to wake up his little brother and sister, feed them and take them to school, because there were no other family members available. He would not leave his brother and sister to fend for themselves, nor leave them at home where they wouldn't be getting a decent education. So, he chose to be late. Initially he didn't tell anybody, because he thought he could handle it himself. Family is personal. If you don't handle your family problems, you can be perceived as weak in the eyesight of your peers. Tell me, what kind of burden is this for a fifteen-year-old to be carrying?

b. Another kid stopped going to the after-care program. He was a "Crip" gang-member. The after-care program was located in the "Blood" side of the community. He had legitimate concerns about life and death as it pertained to his safety. He chose to be incarcerated and wasn't upset about. He understood why he had to be locked up again. He is still alive and I get it.

c. I love weed. This one got me at first. But, since I've never been an addict, I later understood. One of these kids looked me in my face and told me that he knew he was going to smoke weed when he gets out.

d. Some set aside the Big 3 for something else. Some of these kids are just good actors.

e. And yes, some just fit the description. They are and always will be a criminal. Next question?

# Chapter 21
## Did You Reach All? Sergeant Redd, You Saved My Life

I would definitely say I was able to make a difference in the lives of the majority of the kids who I came in contact with at the facility. I believed that I proved to each kid and staff that I was the exception and not the rule. Yet, was I able to impact them all? I would have to say, no. And, as disappointing as that was, I would not let that stop my tenacity to press on. You see, as optimistic as I was for the success of every child, I was also realistic about the fact that everybody was not going to make it. So regardless of my suspicions or doubt about anyone of them, when it would come to them being ready to go home, I always gave everyone my best. I also discovered that at times, I was tougher and spent more time with the knuckleheads than I did with the others. Why? Because I consider myself a knucklehead as well. The people who are the most unlovable are those who need love the most. Sometimes I would try to explain to others my rationale for how I dealt with a particular kid, and I would be told that I was wasting my time. But guess what? Mr. Posey didn't give up on me and I know that I was a knucklehead. I'm so glad that Mr. Posey didn't think that I was a waste of time.

Sending these kids home from this facility and not seeing them again, meant so much to me. Not seeing them again meant they made it. It was very exciting and truly self-satisfying, to hear that kid say with confidence that I would not be seeing them again, and I actually believed him. This particular accomplishment exceeded my wildest expectations. I would then tell them that the best thing they could do for me was to never see them again; at least not see them in here. And based on this knowledge and affirmation alone, I was more than content. But, guess what? The story didn't end there. After being more than content with my feeble attempts to truly make a difference in these kids' lives, something started happening that was nothing short of a miracle. Somewhere between three to six months after these kids left this facility, I started receiving personal phone calls from the same kids who were released from my care. Some of them were no longer in the system at all. I wish I could explain to others what caused this miraculous opportunity to keep reoccurring. Don't get me wrong, one or two calls was understandable, but I would get a call every two weeks from a different kid. Imagine this kid is calling to speak to you to tell you that if it wasn't for you, they would probably have gotten locked up again. Then another kid would call and say, "You saved my life." I'm listening in disbelief as the same young man who I thought was going to end up dead or a career criminal was telling me that some way, somehow my words got through. I still shudder when I think about those phone calls. I kept saying that this can't be happening, but it was.

Until this day, I cannot put into words what those phone calls meant to me. I was able to do more than I could even imagine. I not only helped them, but I helped break the cycle. Mr. Posey helped me and then I helped them. I call it nothing less than a miracle and I am giving God the glory. I was totally clueless. And, if this alone was not enough, the same thing started happening during the weekend visits, with their family.

Visitation for the young men was after lunch on Sundays. The staff would wait for a phone call from the local township, which was about 15 miles away to let us know that visitors were waiting to be picked up and brought to the facility. The trip usually took place at least three times a month. I made this trip numerous times and there were times when other staff made the trip as well. The actual visit took about an hour, maybe an hour and a half. The total time from pick up to returning to the facility was about four hours.

As my popularity and reputation began to grow, I noticed that the following would occur. If I was the person going to pick up the visitors, there would usually be at least one visitor who knew who I was from one of the children or their relatives. To my amazement, I was always receiving accolades and compliments about my abilities and my treatment of the kids. I was speechless. I assured the relatives that I was not just giving them a free ride, but I was also very mindful of my own youthful endeavors and mistakes. I definitely made it clear that I could have been locked up in the same type of place. I felt I had a responsibility to share my overall experience and compel them to rethink their decision-making process. I didn't consider myself someone special.

If these exchanges, in and of themselves weren't enough, on the days when I didn't drive to pick up the relatives, this was the other scenario. Whoever picked up the relatives from the township, would be asked if I was working that day? And if yes, they would want to speak with me. In most cases, I did get to speak with them, but on a few occasions, we were short staffed. These exchanges were priceless. I was being told directly from relatives the impact I was having at the facility and the impact I had in the lives of their next of kin once they had left the facility. These reports just left me speechless and warmed my heart.

# Chapter 22
## He Wasn't Ready or Was He?

I said earlier that there are four separate units in the facility and Unit 4 is the last unit a kid attends before they head back to NYC. One day, one of the kids pulled me aside and told me that he was headed home in two weeks, but he was not ready. First off, this is unheard of. A kid who is about to go home in two weeks ain't telling nobody about his concerns or fears about failing, once he gets back to the block. Nevertheless, this kid told me. Should I report this to the counselor? Should I report this to the Psychologist? Forget all that, should I just report it to my supervisor, and go on about my business? I chose, none of the above. I had already experienced what happened when the staff who didn't care about the kids, got a hold of a piece of information about the kids that is precious and how they treated it. I can only describe the outcome as ugly. This kid was about to be set free back into society and he knew that he wasn't ready to depart, but he didn't know how to express it without jeopardizing his own freedom. So, he came to the only person he knew he could trust. He came to the only person in the whole facility who he believed could help him with his dilemma. And, guess what, he was right. But let me be honest. I didn't know I was right at the time. What I did in order to help him, was also a violation of facility policy. I am not proud of that action, but my options were limited. What I did was wrong and I accepted all of the criticism and punishment that came with my actions. If we were teaching these kids to be accountable for their actions, then we should be the example and do the same. So, what did I do that was so wrong? I knew that this kid needed something that would not only reach his mind, but his heart, and his very soul. The question was, "Who among the leaders in the facility was available and capable of fulfilling the three principles?" Nobody. If I, the person he turned too, could personally do that, I knew he had a chance of making it when he left the facility in two weeks. So, I did what I do well, and could possibly make a difference. I wrote him a poem. You did what? That's right. I said it. I wrote him a poem. Here is what is interesting. I told him that I needed to travel to Baltimore over the weekend, but when I returned in a few days, I was going to have a present for him. I told him to hold out and don't do anything stupid until I returned on Monday. When I returned on Monday, I read and gave him a copy of the poem that I had written especially and personally for him. Guess what? It accomplished exactly what I wanted it to accomplish. And, in two weeks, he was ready physically and mentally to go home. This might seem very minor to some, and no big deal. Technically, I should have gotten permission and approval, before I executed it. Previously, I mentioned that it is easier to ask for forgiveness, than permission. This is one of those examples. But my actions, in this case, cost me far more than I had anticipated at the time I felt compelled to help this young man out. (Note: I talk about this in more detail in Book 2. "I Sealed My Fate.")

Having known this kid for almost six months, there were some things I knew about him that I'm not sure he knew about himself. I knew enough to put into words what I knew would rock him at the very core of who he was. I took his past. I took his present. And, then I took his future and showed it to him in one setting, what he was capable of grasping within this dilemma. After I finished reading him this poem, he was in tears. He kept telling me that it fit him to a tee. Can you only imagine how his response and tears made me feel? His next two weeks at the facility were unbelievable. Even the leadership within the facility were commenting on how improved the young man's disposition was. Note: Most of my poetry is in Book 3 of this series, but I had to include this poem here. Enjoy!

# Are You Really Listening?
## (Inspired by "A Kid")

I'm young, gifted and black, and easy to impress.

I know Ja Rule and Fifty-Cent, but tell me, how'd I get into this mess?

Still another man in uniform, yet perpetrating a fraud.

Telling me what is right for me and how to beat the odds.

He only visited my hood on MTV and how I communicate.

Barking on me like some pit-bull, up-state, in this crazy place.

If he just took the time to know me, just to look beyond the mask.

He'd find my hopes and dreams and things I want to last.

He'd learn I love my mother, although I didn't listen.

I say that I don't give a damn, but it's my family, I'm really missing.

And oh yes, I got me a flag and my gang is near the top.

But even if I wanted to quit, tell me, how in the hell am I going to stop?

Why work at Mickey D's, when it won't pay the bills?

And why does corporate America laugh at my attempts? You know that's whacked and ill.

So, if you want to help me, first you've got to know my needs.

If you can't accept me for who I am, don't expect me to succeed.

I'm kicking it to you straight out the ghetto. This here ain't no joke.

Even if I do everything by the letter, I still just might get smoked.

So, step to me correctly, spend a little time down in the hood.

Then when you try to kick it with me, I might just listen like I should,

I might jot down a few notes. Who knows, maybe I'll need to step up my game.

But whether I fail or succeed, things don't have to be the same.

So, when I leave this incarceration and my body is set free.

I don't want to leave behind my mind, I want to take home all of me.

I need to implement a game plan, devoid of doubt and fear.

A concrete solid plan, which all the world can hear.

And when people ask me honestly, how did you ever break the mold?

I'll say I listened to my heart, instead of to everything that I was told.

By

SFC Jerome Redd

March 10, 2003

# Nugget 9: The Long and Short Of It

I have given you the background of Paul. I've given you my background. I've even given you the background of the facility and how it was set up and formulated to reach the kids. The journey now is what Paul was asking for in the beginning. Since I didn't have all of the facts about the kids walking to school nor did I need them, I took you on a one-on-one journey with the kids in Upstate New York. I choose this vehicle for a very specific reason. None of us are the same and no two situations are going to be exactly alike. By providing a variety of different examples, it will assist in giving some insights into what might have been going on at that time. Each situation is different and each situation is unique. The same applies to both groups of people and individuals. You can bring examples, but you can't bring absolutes. When you start determining the present, solely on what you have obtained from the past, you are setting everything and everybody up for failure. Apart from your past, you must make room for input. There has got to be an intake valve somewhere, which allows the flow of new or missed information. I have heard it said before that there are at least two sides to every story and also a third. There is your side. Then there is my side. The third side is the part that neither of us sees, but it still impacts the outcome. Choose what works for you and leave the rest.

# Chapter 23
## We All Need An ROI

Whether the short version or the long version, what truly stands out to me is the fact that you've got to take action. Mr. Posey had insight and he tapped into that insight, but I had to act on it. I did the same thing to the kids in the facility, but they had to act on it as well. Insight without action is just knowledge. In order for knowledge to be worth something, you have to do something with it. Life in and of itself is a struggle. There is no getting around the struggle and there is no getting around life. Let your actions be productive. Let your actions bring something in return.

What is your ROI (Return On Investment)? Those kids who were headed to Catholic school, and the kids who were harassing them were all looking for the ROI. Boarding the kids at the local school was an alternative. It was not a solution. And, too many folks quit, because the search is far too great. You've got to search, process, then react. This affords you the ability to achieve or to at least move forward. The individuals involved have to make the difference. They have to step up and be confrontational, both within and without. Adults can help. Outside sources can even assist. But, the true answers lie within. We can be the example. We can set the example. We can even stir them up. But we can't give them the answer. They have to reach within and find it for themselves. Our time with them is only for a moment, a season, a life-time, but they still must rise to the occasion.

"When we fail to let them fly; when we fail to push them out of the nest; we might as well just clip their wings. They will never fly; they will never soar, they will never truly achieve, until they jump." (Author: Steve Harvey).

Brokenness is a part of life. You don't get to hide from it. You don't get to avoid it. And, you definitely don't get to ignore it. It has its own unique signature and that signature is usually ugly. I tell folks all the time that I am blessed and highly favored. Because I was fortunate enough to recognize and address my brokenness, before it was too late. Thank you, Mr. Posey. Thank you, Army Major Chaplain. Thank you, Mr. & Mrs. Albert and Nina B. Redd (My Parents). And thank you God, for the major role that all of them played in and on my life. Also, thank you for allowing me to show and share that impact on the incarcerated kids and now on the world.

When I first started writing this book, it went from one book to three. When I was nearly finished with the first one, I knew that I had a problem on my hands. There was too much to put into just one book. My wife asked me was there going to be more? I told her that it's coming. There are those who have survived the cycle and have broken the chains. I am humbled and I am proud to have been such a part of a profound outcome. I got to see this personally and even heard back from some of them while I was still working at the facility. In my heart of hearts, I believe that some of them are going to read this book and are going to recognize that I am their Mr. Posey. Notwithstanding, some of them are no longer in the system, but thriving. I want to believe that they will read this and then reach out to me, as one of them has already done on social-media's Facebook. And like Paul Harvey, they will give me the rest of the story. I guess I'm going to have to write another book. Who knew? Good-day.

Be on the lookout for Books 2 & 3 of this series. As you can see, Book 1 gave you background and showed you how Jerome handled the one-on-one and group sessions with the kids. He also gave you examples of the different tools he had in his tool-box. Book 2 will show the difficulties, frustrations and objectives that Jerome had to confront and navigate on this journey, without becoming a casualty himself. It also gives hope, inspiration and guidance to those who have embraced the tough job of dealing with the broken. Book 3 is a blessed example of the potential rewards that can result when you decide to go all in and make a difference.

# Connect With Me
# Contact Information For Jerome Redd

Website: www.letsthinkchangegrow.com

Email: jredd@letsthinkchangegrow.com

Email: glasspoetry@gmail.com

Facebook: https://www.facebook.com/jeromeromey.redd/

Twitter: https://twitter.com/JeromeRedd

https://www.instagram.com/jeromeredd7/

https://www.linkedin.com/in/jerome-redd-a936b64/

www.ingramcontent.com/pod-product-compliance
Lightning Source LLC
Chambersburg PA
CBHW051615010526
44107CB00037B/1435/J